The Bearsden Secret Society Mountaineering Club

ANDREW VICKERY

Publication Data

Published by BSSMC Publications
andyv4@btinternet.com

First Published May 2012

ISBN 978-0-9572774-0-3

Printed by Kelso Graphics, Kelso.

Acknowledgements

I wish to thank all those who have taken part in The Bearsden Secret Society Mountaineering Club's annual get togethers over the years and those who have lent their support to participants. Particular thanks must go to Tom Sharpe for his contributions to this account, his assistance with editing and his photographs. Thanks also to Graham Freeland for photographs, to Douglas Whitie for advice and to all at Kelso Graphics who brought this long term project to life. Finally, thanks to the late Dan Livingstone for his inspiration.

Lord Berkeley's Seat on An Teallach

Foreword

"Mountaineering is not a dangerous pursuit and it has many facets, any one of which could arouse a life-long interest." – Dan Livingstone 1967

"The Bearsden Secret Society Mountaineering Club" is about a small group of friends who, through a shared interest in mountaineering, have enjoyed enduring friendships over a period of 42 years. Its exploits are legendary, at least in the minds of the six or so people involved. Its origins are in Rutherglen, a Royal Burgh to the southeast of Glasgow, although it has become more geographically diverse over the years.

It is not about Bearsden, it is not about a secret society and the numbers involved hardly justify use of the word "Club" (which implies a degree of organisation), but there is at least a notion of mountaineering. While the thread of climbing, or "compleating" all the Munros (Scottish mountains over 3000 feet high) runs through this light hearted account of annual reunions, it is certainly not a guidebook.

"Frien'ship mak's us a' mair happy,
Frien'ship gi'es us a'delight;
Frien'ship consecrates the drappie,
Frien'ship brings us here tonight.
Happy we've been a' thegither,
Happy we've been ane an' a'
Time shall find us a' the blyther
When we rise to gang awa'." – Robert Burns

Mountaineering is not a dangerous pursuit......!

Contents

The Inaccessible Pinnacle, the Cuillin, Skye

Chapter 1

Pre-Natal Development

While it may not have been apparent at the time, the Bearsden Secret Society Mountaineering Club (usually referred to as the BSSMC to maintain the element of secrecy) was conceived in 1966, when a decision was taken by staff at Rutherglen Academy, inspired by the Depute Rector at the time, Dan Livingstone, to purchase a disused schoolhouse in Inveralligin on the north shore of Loch Torridon for conversion to an outdoor centre to be used by pupils from the school. Dan had, for many years, led groups of pupils on expeditions to the Cairngorms during school holidays and some had gone on to join him on summer trips to the Pyrenees. He held a strong belief that outdoor activities had an important part to play in education and with a permanent base in an area of outstanding mountain landscape he could envisage this extending to field trips to study geography, geology, biology and social history. His vision was to have a major impact on many pupils of that era.

Three such pupils were Roderick MacKenzie, George Rhind and Andrew Vickery, who were all in their second year at the Academy at the time. The early stages of purchase and development of the Outdoor Centre involved pupils who were slightly older, but they could not escape the numerous fund raising projects which were taking place on an almost daily basis. As Inveralligin momentum grew, so did their interest, albeit via routes outside school to some extent.

George already had an interest in outdoor activities from being in the Boy Scouts, although his conversations about the merits of the "Back-Woodsman's" Badge were lost on Boys' Brigade lads Roderick and Andrew. So when he was presented with the opportunity to visit Inveralligin he was supremely confident in his ability to meet every challenge on offer.

As a member of the 204th Glasgow Company of the Boys' Brigade, Andrew had become involved in the BB's Expedition Badge programme. Preparing for his first expedition in 1968, he demonstrated a completely un-informed, yet adamant, commitment to an interest in mountaineering by embarking on an expedition of a more serious nature – to purchase a suitable pair of boots. He had persuaded his father, keeper of funds, to take him to Millett's Store, a cheap but adequate supplier of outdoor equipment, to seek out appropriate footwear. He tried on several pairs of boots, all at the cheaper end of the range. He was, however, attracted to a slightly more expensive pair and set to work persuading his father that these were the boots he really needed. Eventually he succeeded in coaxing a reluctant wallet from his father's pocket, not an easy task, along with the remark, "Well, I hope you're going to use these." Mr. V. would be pleased to know that some 44 years and many pairs of boots later, Andrew often suffers from blisters similar to those he first encountered in these boots, but still struggles out on the hills as often as he can. That first pair of boots disintegrated finally during an overly rapid descent of the stone chute on Liathach in Torridon on a hot summer's day some years later.

Having become the proud owner of a pair of adequate walking boots and protected from the Scottish weather by a nylon anorak and a borrowed, bright yellow cycling cape, Andrew's introduction to the mountains of Scotland was a cold, wet weekend of 30th April / 1st May 1968, when he and two fellow BB boys from the 204 camped at the edge of a wood below the shoulder of Beinn Dubhchraig near Tyndrum.

The next significant stage of pre-natal development came soon after, on a late spring weekend in 1968, when Andrew and George visited Inveralligin for a three day "Geography Weekend", led by their geography teacher, Jim Cathcart. Jim was to become the second influential figure in the development of the group's interest in the mountains. The long weekend consisted of geography "fieldwork", several lectures - well, chats really - on the geology and social history of the area and, more significantly, a full traverse of the ridge of Beinn Alligin.

Meanwhile, Roderick was involved in a similar process of persuading his father of the necessity to purchase a pair of boots in preparation for a two week summer trip to Inveralligin in 1968. During this trip Roderick climbed his first mountain, Beinn Dearg, at 2999 feet only one foot short of 914 metres – the magic point at which a mountain may be defined as a "Munro". This was, perhaps, an early sign that Roderick would not be drawn, later, into the business of "Munro bagging".

So, Andrew, George and Roderick had been well and truly bitten by the mountaineering bug. Between 1968 and 1970 they spent many of their school holidays at Inveralligin, including a memorable Christmas in 1968 when the three first ventured out on a hill together (Beinn Alligin), under the leadership of Dan Livingstone and Jim Cathcart. Dan had retired in 1968 to live permanently in Inveralligin, where he had built a house with much help from Murdo the local boat builder, the brute strength of some former pupils and the willing assistance of pupils who would fetch and carry during "work party" visits to Inveralligin, the main purpose of such visits being to carry out maintenance work at the centre.

A further significant development in 1968 was the arrival of a new teacher at the Academy, Bill Brown, a former pupil himself. Bill brought further enthusiasm and depth - and his car - to the small group of teachers who gave much of their free time to taking pupils to the hills.

Andrew left the Academy in 1970, with George and Roderick leaving the school (by then Cathkin High School in Cambuslang) the following year.

By then, a broad group of teachers, former and current pupils had formed a mountaineering pool, of varying skills, experience and ability, which met most weekends and during school holidays to walk and climb. Inveralligin remained a focal point, while BB expeditions, in which Andrew and Bill were involved, served to enlarge the group. Various groups assembled for days on the hills within striking distance of Rutherglen, relying in those early days on transport provided by Jim, Bill and their generation of mountaineering friends. To some of the younger members of the group the cars themselves were good reason to go to the hills, the star attraction being Jim's Lancia Fulvia, with curtains on the rear window - armchair comfort and fast too! The bar in the Cambus Court Hotel in Cambuslang became the basecamp from where routes for the weekend were planned as the group continued to develop and thrive.

Meanwhile, another pupil at Rutherglen Academy, Tom Sharpe, was being initiated into the delights of Inveralligin on a geography weekend in the spring of 1970 again led by Jim Cathcart. Lacking suitable equipment, Tom and others in the group were kitted out with boots and orange cagoules manufactured by Blacks of Greenock, recently acquired by the school. It is highly likely that an ascent of Beinn Alligin was part of the weekend.

Tom's mountaineering experience was furthered, if that is the appropriate term, two years later when, as a young BB officer in the 187th Glasgow Company, he attended a weekend "Expedition Training Course", later described by Tom as "a shambles", at the BB's Officer Training Centre at Carronvale. Mountain safety experts will be thrilled to hear that Tom's zip-up ankle boots with smooth soles were considered suitable footwear for his BB supervised weekend on the Ochils, along with his plastic pac-a-mac as "waterproof" clothing. The torrential rain of the weekend left Tom with laryngitis and a week off school.

Unperturbed, he went on to teach the expedition class as part of the Duke of Edinburgh Awards Scheme and he arranged an expedition for his group in the Balquhidder area. Bill Brown was enlisted as assessor and, on Saturday 26th August 1972, while he and Tom viewed the group's progress from the summit of Creag Mhor, Bill mentioned that the following weekend he and Andrew Vickery were going to climb Ben More at Crianlarich and invited Tom along. So, the next date of significance in the pre-natal development of the BSSMC was 2nd September 1972, when Bill, Andrew and Tom met up at Crianlarich to climb Ben More and Stobinian. This was the first time Tom and Andrew had met, although it was to emerge later that they were related, very distantly through marriage.

By this time, Tom had acquired more appropriate footwear than his zip-up town boots. He had gone through the routine visit to an outdoor equipment shop with his father to purchase "proper" boots. In Tom's case the shop in question was Roberts Stores, on Trongate in Glasgow, where

Bill Brown had worked while he was a student and which he promoted shamelessly to budding mountaineers at Rutherglen Academy. Despite his new boots, a very hot, humid day and the unrelenting slope of Ben More, a very red faced Tom was undeterred and soon became a regular participant in the group's activities.

In summer 1973, Andrew and George made an early attempt to introduce the idea of an annual expedition when, with three friends, Alistair Corbett, Gordon Craig and David Stirling, they took off with a large frame tent on a Great North Tour, taking in Fort William, Ullapool, Bettyhill and Helmsdale. Although three mountains were climbed, fishing was a more popular, less strenuous activity and the consumption of frequent, copious quantities of alcohol was, by far, the most popular activity of the week. Some of those involved still shudder at the thought of their "Helmsdale Hangovers" and to this day the BSSMC has never dared set foot again in that town, despite changes in personnel and a much more responsible attitude to alcohol.

1974 saw Andrew and Derek Osborne venture abroad for the first time – to the Lake District for a long weekend over Easter, followed by a two week expedition to the Pyrenees, with Bill Brown as driver and guide. Sales of Bachelor's Savoury Rice have never again reached the peak of that year. The idea of an annual trip continued in 1975, when Andrew, Roderick and Gordon Craig camped at the National Trust campsite at the head of Loch Duich from where they climbed several mountains in Kintail. 1976 and 1977 brought further overseas trips, when Andrew and Roderick made expeditions to the Stubai Alps in Austria and the Atlas Mountains of Morocco, under the umbrella of the Ramblers' Association.

Meanwhile, Tom's regular walking partner was Donald McNeill, with whom he was tackling many of the Loch Lomond and Arrochar hills. Ben Lomond was a particular favourite, Tom and Donald often being accompanied by Dorothy Brebner and Catriona Milne in those days. In 1974 Tom and Donald completed the famous route round the main ridge on Arran, where Tom's love affair with granite began. Together they also had memorable ascents of Beinn Bhuide, where they came close to being terminally singed by a nearby lightning strike, Ben Lui with 30 lb packs en route from Tyndrum to Dalmally and frequent visits to the hills near Tyndrum where the McNeill family stayed in a cottage at Auch.

Tom and Donald's most memorable day trip in the mid 1970s was from Glen Doll Youth Hostel, taking in Mayar, Dreish, Lochnagar and the outlying hills of the White Mounth in a 10½ hour multi-Munro 25 mile marathon, their progress being monitored regularly by the hairy wee warden at the hostel, a really caring fellow who was interrogating incoming hostellers about the progress of the two young Munro baggers.

Like many a Rutherglen Academy senior pupil, Tom was introduced to whisky at Inveralligin during a short visit with Bill Brown. They had called in to see Murdo and Peggy Macdonald – Murdo had been the skilled tradesman in the renovation of the Field Centre as well as the builder of Dan's house. Peggy was renowned for pouring very large drams of "Quosh" – the undiluted spirit which appeared mysteriously from the distillery in Quosh soft drink bottles. She kept this under the sink beside the bleach and washing-up liquid. Plied with a full tumbler of cask strength whisky, Tom recalls little of his dinner at Peggy's that evening other than it involved a deer which had had an "accident".

Throughout those early years, the Cambus Court Hotel continued to act as base camp as the group enlarged. Firm friendships were cemented, new friendships developed and the Bearsden Secret Society Mountaineering Club foetus was developing slowly, although a delivery date remained uncertain but some way off.

Chapter 2

The Inaugural Annual Expedition

By the late 1970s the group of Rutherglen Academy former pupils who had spent so much time together at Inveralligin and on day trips from Rutherglen had begun to move away from the area. Roderick had moved to Manchester and was inspecting taxes, his employer offering little likelihood of an early return to Scotland, if at all. George was doctoring, or whatever junior doctors did between bouts of partying and subsequent hangovers, spending short spells in a variety of hospitals round the U.K. as he learned his trade. Tom was pursuing his career as a geologist at the National Museum of Wales in Cardiff where, having gone to the bother of learning to speak Welsh, he was to make his permanent home. Andrew had married and was settling into a typical domestic regime, spending more time in Tesco than Glencoe and pursuing his career, well, job, in the Department of Social Security, at that time still based in Rutherglen.

On 16th April 1979, Andrew, Roderick and Tom met for a day out on Ben Lawers, the first time they had been out together for several years. Here, a clear commitment was made that they would meet up later that year in an area none of them had visited, so that they could climb some mountains none of them had been up. George was soon included in the plan. They chose Knoydart as their destination. Having heard of how remote the area was, their plan was to walk in to a bothy at Barrisdale, from where several remote Munros (probably the first time the group had used that term consciously) could be climbed.

So, on Saturday 9th June 1979 the BSSMC was born although, like most new born, un-named and oblivious to what the future might hold. Andrew, George, Roderick and Tom met up at their respective "home" bases in Rutherglen and Burnside to set off for Knoydart. At that time, George sported big, bushy hair and a carefully manicured beard. His car was an orange coloured Escort Mexico, his dream car and certainly the most exotic of any in the group since the days of Jim Cathcart's Lancia and its curtains. The two Civil Servants, Andrew and Roderick, were less flamboyant. Roderick had changed little over the years and remained a sobering influence on the others, bringing them back to earth when ideas became a bit fanciful. Andrew often sported a hand-knitted, Shetland wool jumper, which survived for the next twenty five years or so. He supplied the second car in the group, a bright yellow Renault 5, albeit the GTi version. As Tom had changed the length, style and shape of his beard so often over the years it was always questionable whether the others would recognise him. Roderick and Tom travelled as nervous passengers as the two drivers indulged in a "Wacky Race" to Fort William where they met up for a bar lunch in the West End Hotel, which was to become something of a tradition over the following years.

An early afternoon arrival at the road end at Kinloch Hourn saw rucksacks being packed with equipment and food for five days in the hills. Several times during the packing process, George and Tom challenged Andrew about the apparently meagre quantities of food he had planned and purchased in advance of the expedition. His re-assurances were met with some scepticism. Unfamiliarly heavy rucksacks were shouldered and the walk in to Barrisdale Bothy began. It may have been the hot, humid weather, a lack of recent activity or simply premature ageing, but as they made frequent stops along the way, their plans for the week became less ambitious, although no one dared voice such doubts.

A prior arrangement had been made with Dan Livingstone that he would try to meet up with the group at the bothy which, he had assured them, was luxurious by bothy standards, with electricity and running water supplied by the owning estate's home-built hydro electric scheme. Expecting five star accommodation they arrived at the bothy, where Dan was already quite at home. The bothy novices were less than impressed by the makeshift beds and rather suspect looking mattresses while the kitchen fittings were hardly up to the standards they had become used to in their respective levels of domesticity. They were therefore rather relieved and somewhat cheered by the news from a fellow occupant that a group of senior schoolgirls was expected over the next day or so. This presented an opportunity to erect the two Vango Force Ten tents they had carried in and to vacate the suspect beds in favour of the young ladies, who would doubtless be impressed by such chivalry. Alas, the young ladies didn't appear and the young gentlemen therefore felt obliged to share the room with Dan after all.

Two excellent days followed on the three Munros in Knoydart. On the first morning Dan appeared, sporting a red sweatband round his shock of wild white hair, looking considerably fitter than the younger group members. Throughout the day he entertained the group with tales of his mountain adventures in remote, exotic locations, home and abroad. This was fortunate, as the others did not have to try to speak too much between laboured breaths. Dan's only (and oft repeated) regret about his advancing years was that, in an effort to lighten the load in his rucksack, he no longer packed a bottle of whisky and missed his evening dram. Fortunately, the others had had the foresight to pack a half bottle of Grouse, naively considered more than enough to satisfy the needs of four or five thirsty mountaineers for the best part of a week, which they had managed to keep out of Dan's sight. On the second night, after dinner, Dan was presented with a dram, albeit a fairly meagre one. The look of surprise and delight on Dan's face gave his protégés great pleasure. It was to be the last time Dan would be part of the group, but his enthusiasm and guidance during the BSSMC's formative years will never be forgotten and his presence during that first annual expedition was an inspiration.

One problem which re-emerged on the first day at lunch time, following the previous day's expressed doubts, was Andrew's distribution of food to the others, who questioned whether two squares of Cadbury's Dairy Milk and a handful of raisins really constituted a lunch. His assurances regarding the sufficiency of the carefully calculated rations were met by scarcely concealed scepticism, again. Of course, no one starved which suggests that the doubters may have been exaggerating the issue.

After two successful days Dan left the bothy to return home, while the others packed the tents and walked over to Lochan nam Breac, a remote and, depending on one's outlook, either idyllic or midge ridden camp site. An attempt to climb Sgurr na Ciche the next day was aborted in rain and low cloud and the group retreated to the tents. As the rain eased, attention focused on keeping the midges at bay. An open campfire – George's Back Woodsman's Badge was finally proving useful – and copious quantities of pipe smoke, generated by George and Tom, helped to restrict the midges to tolerable levels. Sadly, dissent within the group continued, as war broke out over allocation of the final few raisins and the remaining crumbs of chocolate. This soon became a matter of survival. When counting out the raisins for the next day's rations, Andrew accidentally dropped a few on the floor of the tent. George and Tom pounced on them, stuffing them into their mouths before Andrew could insist on their return. Roderick resisted being drawn into the undignified melee. Of course, no one complained about how light the rucksacks had become once the carefully calculated rations had been consumed, although that may simply have been a reflection of how little had been packed in the first place. Over subsequent years, stories of "The Knoydart Rations" became much exaggerated, according to Andrew, but the tale quickly assumed the status of the first and possibly greatest BSSMC legend.

After a return to Barrisdale to dry out (- no connection with the now drained half bottle), the group walked out to Kinlochourn and pitched the tents beside a midge-infested burn not far from the Tomdoun Hotel. Initial attempts to find the public bar failed as the group was put off, far too easily, by the fact that the apparent entrance to the bar was through a corrugated iron porch which was occupied by a large number of rather noisy, roosting chickens. A second attempt proved that this was, in fact, the entrance and that in true bar room fashion, the chickens just had to be pushed aside to reach the bar, which was little more than a hatch through to a residents' lounge. On purchasing drinks they soon learned that while they had been in the isolation of Knoydart there had been a budget and the price of beer had gone up. Over a meal in the hotel they also learned

Rutherglen Academy Field Centre, Inveralligin (1977)

Dan Livingstone on Ladhar Bheinn

Shenavall Bothy (centre of picture) and the mountains of Fisherfield

Badanaiska in 2010

Loch Ossian Youth Hostel

Loch Treig from Stob Coire Sgriodain

Culra Bothy

Great Glen from Meall nan Dearcag, SW of Laggan

Not The West Highland Way

The West Highland Way

that, despite, or perhaps because of its rather quaint state of dilapidation, the hotel had been used recently by an eccentric, elderly gentleman whose habit of wearing makeup and a nightcap as he was served breakfast in bed, had fascinated the younger, female members of staff in particular. The gentleman in question was none other than W.A. Poucher, author and famous mountain photographer. Some years later, George came across him in a hospital, still wearing his makeup in bed.

At Tom's request, a detour was made on the return journey to Rutherglen, to Glen Roy, to afford him the opportunity to look at the Parallel Roads. Making side trips to view significant geological sites was to become a feature of many future expeditions but, at least until Tom's friend and fellow geologist Alastair Macrae joined the group some years later, the level of interest shown by the others was, at worst nil and at best, apathy.

And so the precedent for an annual expedition had been set and plans were made for a similar trip the following year. Almost subconsciously, a Munro list was being compiled and ticks were being entered, at least by two members of the group, but in those early days the priority remained getting a small group together once a year to maintain a link with past happy days on the hills and to explore other parts of Scotland in the future.

Chapter 3

Shenavall

For a number of years Roderick had been suffering from ankylosing spondylitis and by 1980 this was affecting his mobility, so he was using his summer holidays to attend a clinic for some treatment and was therefore unavailable for the 1980 expedition. On 12th July it was just Andrew, George and Tom who met up in Rutherglen for a trip to Ullapool. Having been introduced to the idea of using bothies the previous year, they had decided to use Shenavall bothy in the heart of the "Whitbread Wilderness" in Wester Ross, from where a number of very remote Munros could be tackled. George was still driving his Escort Mexico, while Andrew had acquired a black Alfasud. One should pause at this point to spare a thought for other drivers on the road to Ullapool that day.

On their arrival at Ullapool the trio booked into a bed and breakfast establishment – even in those early days there was no great enthusiasm for roughing it unnecessarily. This was the first year for which accounts were kept, a rather complicated system of topping up a kitty, with records of contributions and expenditure being kept in an old, blue covered school jotter, pinched from Rutherglen Academy some years earlier. The records show that this first night's B&B cost £15 for three.

Next day the group spent a day on nearby Beinn Dearg. Having reached the summit, George and Tom took in the outlying Cona' Mheall while Andrew waited at the bealach, partly because of his immediately apparent lack of fitness and partly due to early signs of blisters, a recurring problem. The return was made over Meal nan Capraichean, which was generally referred to as Mull Nan Capricorn by the sadly Gaelic deficient group members (although, as a Welsh speaker, Tom has always made an effort at correct pronunciation). On their return to the cars, a majority decision saw the group depart that same evening for the walk in to Shenavall bothy, rather than wait until the next day, which would have been a much more sensible approach given the poor physical condition of the oldest member of the group.

It was a late evening walk in, with full packs containing food for about three days. Andrew, despite the harsh criticism of his victualling the previous year, had retained his position as quartermaster. In response to the criticism he had increased the amount of food to be carried which, of course, resulted in ridiculously heavy rucksacks. As the landrover track deteriorated into a sketchy path leading further into the "Wilderness" the group conjured up images of remote camp sites and lone campers seeking solitude. The person whose name sprung to all three minds was Jimmy Jamieson, a geologist friend of Jim Cathcart's, who had been a regular visitor to Inveralligin in the 1970s. Jimmy had made several trips to Antarctica and while back home in Scotland his specialist subject seemed to be "Remote Places In Which I Have Spent a Week In a Tent". Although he was something of a loner, perhaps having spent too much time with penguins, he was much admired for his exploits in Antarctica and even more remote places in Scotland.

As the group approached the bothy in fading light it was evident that it was already fairly fully occupied. Bodies were coming and going and concern began to grow that there would be no room at the inn, particularly as someone had already pitched a small tent some distance from the bothy and was brewing up as the group drew nearer. None other than Jimmy Jamieson!! Spooky or what? Greetings were exchanged briefly before Andrew, George and Tom took occupation of the loft platform inside the bothy, entered by a ladder through an open hatch, the ground floor being fully occupied. The loft floor was soon strewn with sleeping bags, cooking equipment, food and enough gear to have seen out a season in Antarctica with the aforementioned Jimmy. The open hatch presented a fairly serious hazard to the group as they weaved their way through the debris in the confined space of the loft.

14th July was a dull but hot, sticky day. The chosen hills for the day were A'Mhaighdean and Ruadh Stac Mhor which, as with most routes to the hills from the bothy, involved a fairly serious river crossing – a particular nuisance to those whose feet had to be protected against developing blisters by a variety of plasters and tape. Training shoes were used for the fording and left at the other side for the return. A long day in the heat did little to help Andrew's blisters or Tom's increasingly painful knee, which was to become his Achilles Heel over many years, so they both put themselves at the mercy of Dr. George that evening. This they came to regret later as Dr. George took the opportunity to practise his surgical techniques on the blisters and his dispensing skills with a fine variety of brightly coloured tablets, whose names he pretended to know.

The following day brought kinder weather. To his great credit, George, the fittest member of the group by far, offered his services as a human ferry for the river crossing, as he nursed the walking wounded on the long walk in to Beinn Tarsuinn. At the summit, which happened to be Andrew's 100th Munro (yes, by now he was counting), a slightly bizarre, semi-pre-arranged meeting took place with a doctor friend of George's from Ullapool, who could be seen from above approaching the hill across a never-ending peat bog, accompanied by his St. Bernard dog, before joining the others at the summit. Sadly the St. Bernard did not carry a barrel of brandy, or indeed a stretcher, which would have been of use later in the day, as it transpired.

Leaving the doctor and his dog behind for their return trip across the peat bog, the others set off for the long ridge walk over three further Munros and back to Shenavall. The blisters were unhappy at their continuing incarceration inside Andrew's boots and Tom's knee was objecting to further use, to the extent of threatening industrial action. Finally, on rough ground between the final two summits, Tom's knee gave up the ghost and locked, causing him to keel over and fall to the side in an amazingly accurate impersonation of Del Boy's famous fall in "Only Fools and Horses", accompanied by a yelp of pain from the injured Sharpe. Dr. George to the rescue again, this time with an even more brightly coloured variety of pills which, almost as soon as they had been administered, seemed to make Tom extremely happy and quite forgetful. He remembered very little of the return trip to the bothy, even his fits of laughter as he was transported across the river by his trusty mount, George. He slept particularly well that night. And Dr. George wasn't struck off!

After retreating from Shenavall the next day, the group booked into a newly opened, very comfortable, privately run bunkhouse at Dundonnell for a couple of nights, where they enjoyed the luxury of bunk beds and hot, running water. Despite a rest day, Andrew's blisters were in no state to allow him on to the hills on the 18th, so George and Tom went off for a day on the northern summits of the Fannichs, while Andrew nursed what was left of his feet. His sole (pun intended) contribution to the day was to have tea brewing by the side of Loch Droma, from where he could see George and Tom making their descent from the hill late in the afternoon.

For some unrecorded reason, but probably something to do with the growing urge to "bag" as many Munros as possible while expending as little effort as they could, the group moved to Newtonmore on the 19th, taking in a couple of easy A9 Munros before booking in to yet another B&B (only £12 for the three this time). The B&B provided a convenient base camp for the 200 yard walk to the Glen Hotel (distances to pubs were still measured in yards then) for a decent meal. This may have been the pilot annual BSSMC dinner, but accounts of it are vague, memories dulled by copious quantities of Glenfarclas 105 proof and cigars!

The following morning, hangovers fought a ferocious battle with full cooked breakfasts, as three pale faced young men tried to display a sober, presentable image to the landlady, who was probably well aware of their antics the night before. Nevertheless, determination to enter even more ticks on the Munro list resulted in an easy ascent, although in wind and rain, of one of the forgettable A9 summits, A'Bhuidheanach Bheag, which straddles the boundary of two counties, Inverness-shire and Perthshire, the boundary being marked by the remains of a fence. Andrew explained that one of his work colleagues refused to believe that such boundaries on the map were often marked by fences on the ground so Andrew, in a fair impression of King Arthur, ripped one of the metal fence posts from its foundations, used it as a walking stick and finally transporting it back to his office to accost the aforementioned sceptic.

It was during these two days at Newtonmore that Gore-Tex made its first appearance in the BSSMC. George was the proud owner of a new Gore-Tex jacket, being the only person who could afford such an item in those days. Much to his annoyance, however, the early design of these jackets contained one major flaw – the Gore-Tex label was stitched directly on to the front of the jacket and let in water through the stitched seam, a flaw which manufacturers soon resolved.

Sadly, this was to be the last annual meeting to be attended by George. His administration of pain killers and his selection of state of the art surgical tapes and plasters have never been forgotten. Given that he finally became a Consultant Geriatrician, it is hoped that his expert services will not be required by group members for a while yet.

Approaching Shenavall Bothy

Chapter 4

And Then There Were Two

The Summer Expedition

As George had, to a large extent, traded in his boots for his stethoscope by 1981 and Roderick was spending another summer having further treatment to his back, it was just Andrew and Tom who kept the tradition of the annual expedition alive. As it turned out there was to be a second expedition that year, but they didn't know that when they set off from Rutherglen on 31st May. By now, Andrew had moved to Newcastle and rising mortgage costs had led to him driving a rather more sedate car, a grey Renault 14, which he and Tom packed with more than enough luggage for their journey to Boat of Garten. Bill Brown owned a permanently sited caravan there and had kindly agreed to make it available for the week. Records do not show whether any payment was ever made to Bill. Perhaps the absence of the "Taxman" led to incomplete record keeping or perhaps Andrew and Tom were just too mean to have paid Bill.

An "A9 Munro", Carn na Caim, provided an easy breaking-in day before Andrew and Tom were joined by Cathy Millar, a university friend of Tom's, now living in Inverness and working at the museum there. The BSSMC appears to have been an exclusively male domain to date so it was a significant development for the males to be joined by Cathy. On 1st June the trio used the Cairngorm chairlift (Oh dear!) to access the plateau before walking out to Macdui. They carried heavy packs as it was their intention to descend to the Lairig Ghru, spend the night in one of two bothies en route, or maybe even just bivouac, before crossing Braeriach. There seems to have been a sort of a plan. Whether the plan failed because of the off-putting, filthy interiors of the huts or the threat posed by developing thunder storms, is unclear. Anyway, the final outcome was a rather pathetic retreat to the upper car park on Cairngorm via the Chalamain Gap, making the carrying of all sorts of cooking equipment, food and so on a rather pointless exercise. Evidence was mounting to suggest that the two founder members were getting a bit too soft for "real mountaineering".

With Cathy having returned to Inverness, Andrew and Tom set off for one of the "easy" A9 Munros, Meall Cuaich. A wet walk in along a good track led to a bothy which provided shelter for an early lunch. Looking out of the bothy window, past an empty whisky bottle on the sill, Andrew and Tom could see only cloud and rain where the mountain ought to have been. The bothy was reasonably comfortable but after about an hour and a half staring at the whisky bottle, wishing there had been some whisky in it, Andrew and Tom abandoned their plan and retreated to the car.

Fortunately, the next day brought slightly better weather and Andrew and Tom had a good, long day out on a full traverse of the Glen Feshie hills, which, in those days, had a few more Munros than now. This was followed by an enjoyable meal in the Lynwilg Hotel, where the favoured choice from the menu was "Steak Rob Roy", the key element being a whisky sauce. Another good day on Creag Pitridh followed before a rest day was called for.

Andrew and Tom had been introduced to the delights of Macallan Single Malt Whisky during their days in the Cambus Court Hotel so, with the Macallan Distillery not too far away, they decided to pay it a visit. The distillery was not open to the general public at that time and production had stopped for the annual summer holiday and maintenance programme. Nevertheless, the two distillery managers who were present made the pair very welcome for a blether in the office. As they chatted, one of them scratched his head, thinking if there might be anything of interest with which to entertain the visitors.

"Do we have any of the new Royal Wedding bottles around yet?" he asked his colleague.

"Aye, the first bottle's in the safe", was the reply.

With that he unlocked the safe and produced a bottle of a new Macallan which had been specially vatted to commemorate the forthcoming marriage of Prince Charles to Diana Spencer. It contained whisky from just two casks, one from Charles' year of birth and one from Diana's year of birth and was the first of a very limited edition. He handed the bottle to Andrew and Tom who couldn't believe their luck.

On taking it back the distillery manager asked, "What do you think of this, then?"

Andrew and Tom mumbled a few complementary and appreciative words, anticipating the sample dram which seemed certain to be poured, before the bombshell was dropped –

"Good, that's about as close as you're likely to get to tasting it. I doubt if many of the bottles will be opened, they're probably just going to be bought as investments by collectors."

The bottle was returned to the safe and the four settled down to a more mundane, but still very welcome, glass of Single Malt.

Next day, a fairly quiet, well behaved week ended with a successful return visit to Braeriach.

The Autumn Expedition

With very little forward planning, a second get-together was arranged between 30th August and 4th September, involving Andrew, Roderick and Tom. The weather that week was unusually hot and humid and the hills climbed were not particularly memorable in themselves. However, the week is remembered well by those involved because of other experiences.

Looking for easy access to Beinn a'Cleidh, an outlier of Ben Lui, the group decided to drive up a long farm road and seek permission to leave a car at the farm, rather than face a long walk in to the hill. Roderick lost the toss of a coin and it was his very recently acquired Fiat which was subjected to the rigours of a very rough farm road and an even rougher greeting from several, very large, slobbering hounds (dog lovers might wish to know that these were of the Doberman variety, but much bigger, more ferocious and more slobbery than normal), which were guarding the farmhouse. Much to Roderick's annoyance and concern, they showed great enthusiasm for examining his car closely, climbing all over it with huge, dirty paws and salivating jaws, trying to eat the wing mirrors for lunch and making a fine job of taking the new look off the paintwork. Andrew was nominated to leave the relative safety of the car to make his way over to the farm house to seek permission to leave the car there. With Roderick's face showing a distinct lack of enthusiasm for the car parking arrangements, permission was granted and he reluctantly agreed to leave his pride and joy in the custody of the hounds. Roderick set a fast pace that day.

Later, with Roderick's car more or less intact, apart from dog slobber, the group decided to look for Bed and Breakfast accommodation in the area for the night, with Lochawe the favoured location. The house selected, although how or why the house in question was chosen will remain a mystery (probably cost), was towards the west end of the village, on the opposite side of the road from the loch. Its external appearance should, perhaps, have given a clue as to what lay within. An indistinct path wound through an overgrown garden occupied by free roaming hens, leading to a dilapidated, white-washed house with a wooden balcony supported by several tree trunks. The whitewash was flaking and the blue paintwork was badly in need of attention. A creaking door off a rather exposed balcony led into a dark, sparsely furnished room, which was hall, lounge and dining room in one, with a minstrel gallery above and several doors leading off at both ground and balcony levels. The landlady, who had answered the door rather cautiously, perhaps surprised that anyone was enquiring about accommodation, was a pale, thin, tired looking lady. She showed the three, by then rather apprehensive young men, to basically furnished bedrooms which were of a dubious standard of cleanliness and opened a door to show them a bathroom which was cold, even in the warm weather, and whose fittings were nearing the end of their natural lives. All in all, the accommodation was hardly welcoming and a comfortable stay seemed unlikely but, for some inexplicable reason the trio elected to stay. After all, it was just for one night.

The occupants of the house, whom the group met on returning from the local pub where they had eaten, were interesting. The lady seemed to be the bread winner, eking a living from B&B. Her brother, a large, swarthy fellow who, on first appearance was mistaken for her husband, lingered in the background, checking out the comings and goings of guests. The man who turned out to be the landlady's husband was a small, deaf mute who later in the evening and much to Tom's delight expressed a great interest in photography. Tom was ushered through one of the mysterious doors by the deaf mute to spend an interesting hour or so discussing photographic equipment and comparing notes. Andrew and Roderick opened the door from time to time, just to check that Tom wasn't boring anyone.

Next morning, after a night of hearing every creak and groan of the house, the guests assembled for breakfast. Joining Andrew, Tom and Roderick was a "family" group consisting of a rather eccentric looking cleric or vicar of some description, his "wife" and two quiet children, who were en route to Iona for a retreat. It came as no surprise to learn that this family seemed to be known to, or even related to the owners of the house. Breakfast was served by two children whose presence simply intensified memories of the Addams Family and whose conversation was limited to a description of their daily search through the undergrowth for eggs. Thoughts did turn briefly as to how long the eggs on the plates had been lurking in the overgrown jungle before finding their way to the kitchen. Perhaps it goes without saying that the group left the house with a certain feeling of relief. Over the years, the story of the overnight stay at the house, "Badanaiska" became the second BSSMC legend.

Note: Since 1981 the exterior condition of the house, which has similar legendary status locally apparently, has deteriorated further, with huge gaps in walls where harling has fallen off, rotting window frames and the now totally unprotected balcony gradually collapsing, but still supporting an almost permanent line of washing. The garden is now sufficiently overgrown to attract the combined attention of the two Davids, Attenborough and Bellamy. Sadly, the deaf mute died some years ago but the lady of the house remarried. Her new husband, a forestry worker, apparently tried to renovate the house, but the sheer enormity of the task and a lack of sufficient funds led to defeat and the house is now under threat of demolition from the Local Authority.

Having left Badanaiska behind, the group headed back to Rutherglen via Glencoe, where they set off up the wee Buchaille. Roderick, probably traumatised by events of the previous day, elected to sunbathe by the burn, while the other two scrambled up to the southern top, which was the sole

Munro in these days. Their descent to re-join Rod at the burn meant they did not take in the northern top, later to become a Munro itself.

Having returned to Rutherglen and with Roderick now on his way home, Andrew and Tom drove back up to the Blackmount on 2nd September. En route to one of the outlying summits, Stob a Choire Odhar, they called in at the Inveroran Inn for coffee and to check up on the deer stalking situation. Frank, the waiter who served coffee and scones, was asked about the availability of accommodation for that evening. On his return from making the enquiry elsewhere on the premises, his ensuing explanation left considerable doubt as to whether a room was available or not. Meanwhile, an elderly estate worker who was in the bar at the time advised that it would be wise to check with the gamekeeper about deerstalking. Approaching Forest Lodge to make the enquiry they met the keeper who advised that he wanted everyone to avoid a particular route of ascent direct from the line of the recently opened West Highland Way, to avoid disturbing deer there. Later, taking his advice, Tom and Andrew altered their route and tried to pass on the information to a pair of English West Highland Way walkers, father and son, who were determined to take in the top, walking straight through the area they had been asked to avoid. It was this sort of ignorant disregard for the interests of others which strengthened some BSSMC members' general lack of respect for the W.H.W and those who strayed from it in particular.

Back at the Inn later in the day for a light refreshment after their efforts, they made a further enquiry of Frank, now the barman, about accommodation. This time he came back with a clearer message that the Inn was full but the owner, a very pleasant lady of indeterminate age, appeared and, on learning that Tom and Andrew intended to eat in the Dining Room that evening – no bar meal for these two – offered them the use of a bed settee in her own living room, at no cost other than for dinner and breakfast, an offer gratefully accepted.

Before dinner, non-residents having, for the most part, departed, Frank (barman) and his friend, an estate employee who had graduated to carrying the gun for the stalker, entertained residents with tales of deer stalking, spectacularly accurate shooting and gruesome details of venison butchery, while serving pre-dinner drinks. On entering the Dining Room, dinner was served by Frank (waiter), while Frank (wine waiter) served a well-chilled Beaujolais. When it was suggested that red wine was generally more suited to being served at room temperature, Frank took the wine away and re-presented it later, announcing proudly that he had heated it up on top of the stove. Unfortunately, the temperature of the wine was by now more suited to that of the mulled variety, but Frank was content with his efforts to please the customers. After dinner, in the lounge, now residents' bar, Frank (barman again) served drinks before Frank (musician) played an accordion for the residents to sing and dance the night away.

The residents comprised Tom, Andrew and two elderly couples. Both of the elderly gentlemen had donned full Highland dress for dinner. One was an artist from Fife (apparently well-known, but not to Tom and Andrew) while the other couple hailed from Stranraer. Frank's girlfriend and the hotel owner made up the eight for an eightsome reel.

The bar was so small that one very tightly danced set for an eightsome reel required any non-dancers (so a few others must have been present) to lift feet and legs clear of the action and onto seats. Even so, there were frequent collisions with the furniture, nothing to do with the drink. Eventually, in the early hours of the morning, two rather inebriated BSSMC members retired to the owner's living room while the owner herself wandered through to her bedroom in her night attire. All three slept safely and soundly.

Next morning a very good breakfast was served by Frank (waiter again) before Andrew and Tom packed up reluctantly and set off for another hot day on hills to the north of Loch Awe. Inexplicably, they returned to Rutherglen before heading back north again for a final day in Glen Etive.

This had been an interesting week, well remembered by those present – but not necessarily because of the mountaineering aspects of the trip.

Chapter 5

Glen Affric

The logistics for the 1982 annual expedition were complicated, even although only Andrew, Roderick and Tom participated. The idea was to make use of two cars to facilitate a series of ridge walks into and out of Glen Affric without having to carry food for a whole week. The advantage of meeting up just once a year seems to have been in allowing plenty time for complicated planning!

The expedition began, formally, with lunch at the West End Hotel in Fort William. Each year, usually over a bar lunch or morning coffee en route to the final destination, it had become customary to produce the annual accounts from the previous year and, after rigorous scrutiny, approve them. A resume is then given of the previous year's achievements (or just activities if there had been little in the way of mountaineering) and the current year's annual "meet" is formally opened. This tongue in cheek performance is as close as the BSSMC gets to being anything like a club.

A car was left near the Cluanie Inn before the group drove round to the upper car park in Glen Affric, from where the week began in earnest with a walk into Allt Beithe Youth Hostel, one of the most remote hostels in Scotland.

Next day was warm and humid. The group set off for the hills directly to the north of the hostel, including Sgurr nan Caethreamhnan which, due to a collective ignorance of Gaelic pronunciation, is often referred to as Sgurr nan Chrysanthemum by club members – as it is by many other Munro baggers unwilling to make the effort to learn a wee bit Gaelic. As they ascended the summit ridge of the chrysanthemum, they were aware of a helicopter circling above. They speculated on its purpose – Forestry Commission? Ordnance Survey? National Trust for Scotland? No! Nothing so mundane. As it landed on the ridge just ahead, a gentleman dressed in full Arab dress exited, accompanied by a traditionally dressed Scottish deer stalker. The pilot remained at the controls while a large, swarthy fellow, possibly of Arab origin, stood guard, literally, outside. In his dark suit, white shirt, patterned silk tie and black leather shoes he looked rather out of place at 3000 feet on a Scottish mountain but, as the three nosey mountain walkers approached, he allowed his shoulder holster and handgun to be seen, sending a clear message that this was his territory and that people with boots and rucksacks were the ones who were out of place. He eyed the small group suspiciously but seemed content to allow the pilot to exchange greetings and respond to the group's obvious curiosity. He explained that the Arab gentleman owned the Inverinate Estate and was enjoying a spot of deer stalking. Having located a suitable beast from the air and having used the helicopter to herd it into a convenient position, the "shot" and the stalker had been set down to complete the kill. On completion they would be flown back to Inverinate to celebrate the kill, while the helicopter would return to retrieve the shot beast. After this encounter, the remainder of the day was very ordinary. Thoughts did stray to alternative means of ascending Munros…

Returning to the hostel, the group had a pre-arranged rendezvous with Cathy Niven (formerly Millar), who had kindly offered to bring in and prepare an evening meal, including a bottle of wine which, in those days, was still frowned upon by the SYHA. Fortunately Cathy knew the temporary warden, who joined the group for dinner, which probably made the consumption of wine acceptable. As the group ate, rather well by Allt Beithe standards, another pair at the small table dined on haggis, neeps and tatties. They explained, repeatedly and at great length that they always carried these items on such trips as they could all be cooked in one pot and the water used for tea – yeough! The explanation included not only how all the ingredients could be carried inside one pot, but also how they provided a nutritious, well balanced meal. They probably needed to eat well to have the strength to carry rucksacks full of fresh root vegetables around the country. Another diner, eating the more usual array of dried, packet foods, preferred to talk about his various close shaves during several, rather long falls down Ben Nevis. The group learned later that year that he had died – falling off Ben Nevis. The newspapers did not report whether he had followed the advice of the fellow diners and had been laden down by haggis, neeps and tatties which would certainly have accelerated his fatal fall.

During after dinner chat an interesting club connection began to unravel. The warden brought out the Hostel stamp used to stamp Hostel cards. It was a home made affair, featuring a large, slightly eccentric looking mouse, representing the mouse family which was in permanent residence in and around the hostel and which could make short work of any carelessly stored food. The haggis eaters were confident their dixie could not be penetrated by even such formidable mice. The warden went on to explain that the stamp had been made by the previous year's temporary warden, one Alastair Macrae, who was a friend of Tom's from Glasgow University days (some years later Alastair denied being responsible for making the "mouse" stamp). Alastair's stories of his daily adventures as a warden, including at least one encounter worthy of its own science fiction film, have become legendary, not only in the hostel, but as far away as Glen Cannich.

Next day, Andrew, Roderick and Tom were joined by Cathy for the ascent of Ciste Dubh in warm, sunny weather before spending a third night at the hostel. Then, while Cathy walked down Glen Affric to return home the others walked out to Cluanie over the ridge of Mullach Fraoch-choire and A'Chralaig – another fine day. They used the previously deposited car to return to Cannich Youth Hostel for an overnight stay and restocking of food before returning to Cluanie to walk back in to Allt Beithe, with the other car still in Glen Affric for later use. Complicated enough?

The weather on the walk in should have given a clue that the next day was not going to be fun. Indeed, the 14th of July was a day of low cloud and persistent drizzle, but the logistics of the trip demanded that the walk out to Glen Affric had to go ahead that day. However, why the route over the high summits of Mam Sodhal and Carn Eige remained part of the plan in such weather can be attributable only to the worsening outbreak of Munro bagging disease. The major flaw in this route in such weather was the temptation, to which the group succumbed, to omit the outlying Munro of Bheinn Fhionnlaidh, leaving its ascent as a logistical problem for some years to come.

So it was a wet, bedraggled trio which made a rather later than planned return to Cannich. Too tired to be bothered cooking at the hostel, they hoped they would be able to eat at the Glen Cannich Hotel. Arriving at the hotel at 7.45pm, enquiries were made of the rather severe lady in reception regarding the availability of dinner. Rather haughtily, she explained that service in the dining room stopped at 8pm, but that a bar meal would still be available in the bar. A very quick decision, an unusual BSSMC phenomenon, was made to dine "properly" in the dining room. On communicating this decision to the severe lady, her demeanour changed completely. The 8pm deadline was waived to allow time to clean up and have a well earned pint – there was "no rush, boys." They liked being "boys" and settled down for a very pleasant evening of mothering. Dinner was exceptionally good. Smoked salmon was followed by roast pheasant with game chips and a selection of vegetables. A very tempting sweet trolley was rolled out, bearing several delicious looking desserts. The young waitress gave a full description of each to assist with choice but having already made one quick decision that day, this merely caused confusion and hesitation. Finally, the increasingly tired, but still good humoured, waitress allowed free access to the trolley, to encourage the remaining three, indecisive diners to finish their meals. The trolley was lightened of its remaining load with ease. There was still time for an after dinner dram in the bar before settling the £5.50 per head bill. This meal became recognised over time as the first formal BSSMC dinner and acquired legendary status.

Next morning, as they ate breakfast in Cannich Y.H, Andrew spotted someone he knew from his days in the Social Security Office in Rutherglen. Then she had been a girl who had never really fitted in with colleagues of her own age in the office as her general attitude to life and work was rather too mature for most of the younger staff. Neither had she seemed a likely hill walker or occupant of Cannich Youth Hostel, yet here she was in climbing breeches, pouring over an Ordnance Survey map with a very fit looking young man whom she introduced as her husband. They were serious Munro baggers and far more methodical than the BSSMC. This turned out to be the first of several encounters with them in hostels over a long number of years. Amazingly, the husband went on to be the second person the group had met that week who later went on to make headline news (the first being the chap who kept falling off Ben Nevis). His claim to fame was that, having become lost in whiteout conditions somewhere on the hills above Glenshee, he had dug a snow hole and survived in it for several nights, living off Mars Bars and Irn Bru, until the weather cleared and he was able to walk off the hill into the arms of the mountain rescue teams searching for him. His story seemed to strike a chord with the Scottish press and newspaper photographs of him with cans of Irn Bru must have had the people at Barr's smiling for a while. The couple gave up mountaineering after that and took up ski-ing instead, probably sponsored by Barr's. Later still they turned to mountain biking.

Roderick returned to Rutherglen for a family visit before heading home while Tom and Andrew, having completed their planned hills for the week, drove to Torridon and Inveralligin to re-live their visits to the old schoolhouse some ten and more years earlier. The schoolhouse was no longer a field centre, having been sold by Cathkin High and Stonelaw High Schools due to changing attitudes and increasingly obstructive red tape surrounding outdoor activities as a part of school life. It was now privately owned and conversion work was underway. They left Alligin that day with lumps in their throats – the softies – and spent the night at Torridon Youth Hostel, where they were saddened, when asked to stop talking to allow some young people to hear the television, at the decline in Hostel standards and tradition. It would only be a matter of time before alcohol would be permitted, no doubt!

Leaving the hostel next day before the television viewers were out of their bunks, Andrew and Tom decided to take advantage of good weather to climb three summits next to the Five Sisters of Kintail. Earlier in the week, they had heard the haggis eaters refer to these hills as "The Brothers", but they felt this title had too much of a Hamish Brown (the author who made Munro bagging popular) ring about it and stuck instead to the much more descriptive Aonach Meadhoin, Sgurr a'Bheilach Dheirg and Saileag. Having had enough of hostels for the week the pair treated themselves to dinner, bed and breakfast in Ardochy Lodge, a fine farmhouse near the Tomdoun Hotel and close to the spot where they had camped in 1979.

On their return journey to Rutherglen, they had a walk into the Lost Valley in Glencoe before stopping at the high point on the road across Rannoch Moor, just south of Lochan na h-Achlaise, to walk up the hill to the west of the road. From the summit, on which stands a memorial cairn to Peter Fleming, brother of Ian Fleming, author of the James Bond novels, there are magnificent views across the moor. On a bright, sunny day, this wee hill provided a memorable finish to an excellent week.

Chapter 6

Introducing Alastair D. Macrae

Andrew and Tom met up at Tom's parents' house in Burnside on the morning of 28th July 1983, filled Andrew's car with petrol at a cost of £1.70 per gallon, according to club accounts, and drove to Tyndrum. Waiting for a train at Tyndrum Upper (train being the most efficient way to reach Corrour where accommodation had been booked), Tom passed time by telling a very long joke about someone buying a ticket for a train journey from Wales to China. The joke seemed to set the tone for the week ahead, but is too lengthy to reproduce here. Any reader interested in hearing it should consult T. Sharpe, leaving the remainder of the day free. The train took them from Tyndrum Upper, not to China, but to equally exotic Corrour, from where they walked the short distance to Loch Ossian Youth Hostel. During the train journey and on the walk in, Tom explained that he had made a loose arrangement to meet Alastair Macrae, his friend whose exploits at Glasgow University and as a temporary SYHA warden had gained him a certain notoriety, at least according to Tom's accounts of his adventures. Tom went on at great length to explain how Alastair would bring a whole new dimension to BSSMC expeditions, but that there was no need to include him in plans as he would have "made his own arrangements".

As Andrew and Tom approached the hostel, they spotted a small tent pitched in a midge-infested bog close to a small stand of trees. Tom was absolutely certain this would be Alastair's tent, his preferred accommodation over the fairly cosy building which was the hostel. As they checked in Alastair appeared, announcing he was happy to remain in his tent rather than move into the hostel.

Two enjoyable days on the hills to the north and south of Loch Ossian followed. During the early stages of each day's walk in, Alastair, with only minimal encouragement, recounted tales of his brief career as SYHA warden, confirming his ability to amaze an audience with astonishingly detailed recollections of events which would have passed others by. There was sufficient material for a most entertaining book. Hopefully Alastair will commit his tales to paper before they become exaggerated by the passage of time. He also seemed intent on recounting his entire repertoire of shaggy dog stories and lengthy jokes which easily outshone Tom's rail journey joke, at least in terms of length. Anyone wishing to hear Alastair's jokes and stories should consult A. D. Macrae and leave the rest of the week free.

The route chosen on the second day gave Alastair ample opportunity to entertain – a long ascent of Stob Coire Sgriodain and Chno Dearg via the long ridge of Garbh-bheinn. Somewhere high on the ridge however, Alastair's story telling dried up as he suddenly spotted a tiny, lingering snow patch some 600 feet below. He announced that he needed a cup of tea and, pulling a dixie from his rucksack, he set off on a hasty descent to the snow patch, returning with a dixie full of dirty snow, enough to boil up on his stove to make one cup of tea with lots of dubious bits and pieces in suspension. Fresher water might have come from the lower reaches of the Ganges. Later, as they made their return over Beinn na Lap, Alastair disappeared from sight and was out of contact with the others for a lengthy spell. Assuming he had rushed off to catch a hare for dinner, or perhaps sink a well to find fuel for his stove, Andrew and Tom returned to the hostel. They were surprised to find that Alastair had not beaten them back (the previous day, Alastair had been well in front of the others on the descent – to be found, later, waiting for them with his home made midge shelter, a large piece of fine tea-dyed bridal veil, draped over his upper body) but on this occasion it was to be a while before he appeared. He explained that he had fallen asleep at the summit of Beinn na Lap, suffering from exhaustion, which, he was certain, had been brought on by having been living on freeze dried food and "expedition rations" for a lengthy spell prior to having met up with the others. Fortunately, his recovery was fairly rapid and he was able to join Andrew and Tom by the side of the loch where they enjoyed an after dinner dram, diluted with water from the loch, with only the haunting calls of nearby nesting divers breaking the silence.

Having spent time in a really remote hostel the previous year and in one where television and home comforts were changing standards, Andrew and Tom found the hostel at Loch Ossian the perfect compromise. Its location was remote, yet not far from a railway halt (station would be an exaggeration). Its position at the end of the loch was idyllic, the gas lights and wood panelling creating a cosy, welcoming atmosphere. Water for cooking and washing had to be drawn from the loch by throwing a bucket, attached to a rope, into the loch from the remains of the old pier. They were sorry to be leaving, to return to Tyndrum Upper by train (there is a joke about….), while Alastair left them to walk out to Fort William. The remainder of the week was quiet without him.

Why they decided to drive to Glen Cannich on 1st July is not clear, perhaps they were hoping for a re-run of the previous year's dinner, but they did, stopping at the Onich Hotel for lunch. Over the years, the Onich Hotel would rival the West End Hotel in Fort William in popularity for bar meals and the odd pint.

The following day was not particularly promising weather-wise and Andrew's knee was causing him problems, so a decision was made to have an easy day, making a reconnaissance into Glen Strathfarrar, having heard that access could be difficult. The first obstacle of a locked gate was overcome and a leisurely walk up a path leading to the hills north of the glen was proving pleasant. As lunch was being taken, the weather began to improve so, change of plan – the only place to go was up. As the weather held, good progress was made and what had begun as a gentle day turned into a major Munro bagging exercise, with four in all. Having forgotten about their late start and the repercussions of failing to return through the gate before it was locked for the night, the day ended with a rather faster than was comfortable walk along several miles of the single track road back to the car, leaving the glen just a few minutes before curfew. Unable to resist the temptations of the Glen Cannich Hotel, the pair ate there that night, this time settling for a very good bar meal.

After a well earned rest day, Andrew and Tom drove to Invermorriston where, over coffee in the hotel, they were joined by Cathy Niven, for the third successive year. She had now become more of a regular than one of the founder members. After a late start they enjoyed an excellent day on the four Munros round Sgurr nan Conbharain, culminating with spectacular late evening views from Carn Ghlusaid as clouds tumbled into the valleys below. With Cathy returning home to Inverness, the males made their way back to Glen Cannich for a final night.

The BSSMC consistently failed to record reasons behind most of the strange decisions made over the years, so why Andrew and Tom found themselves driving to Kingussie next day must remain a mystery but the suspicion is that on this occasion, weather forecasts for the east of the country seemed better. After coffee in Fort Augustus, much procrastination, a bar lunch in Kingussie and checking into the Youth Hostel, the weather improved sufficiently for the pair to make a very late start for a quick ascent of Meall Chuaich. There were some raised eyebrows back at the hostel regarding the late start tactics but, given the long hours of daylight offered by summer days in Scotland, the BSSMC often sat out morning rain in a coffee shop, hotel or pub to take advantage of clearing afternoon weather to bag a quick Munro.

On the final day of the 1983 trip there was no need for such delaying tactics, as the day was one of glorious sunshine. Two "A9" Munros provided an easy day on the way home, with time for a final hour's sunbathing, tired feet soaking in the burn.

The week had been memorable for long jokes, an introduction to the unique hillcraft of A.D.Macrae, a couple of excellent hostels, some great days on the hill and some fifteen Munros. This was also the year when BSSMC financial accounts became incredibly detailed. Items such as 36 pence for rolls, 30 pence for bridge toll, even 15 pence for car parking in Pitlochry on the way home, show just how tight this duo had become when it came to ensuring that costs were split evenly. Of more interest, from a social history perspective, is the fact that petrol in Blair Atholl cost £1.77½ per GALLON, while it cost only £1.70 at Burnside. However on 5th July, forced to top up with petrol somewhere between Glen Cannich and Kingussie, the extortionate price of £1.90 per gallon was paid. Common sense must have prevailed though, as only three gallons were purchased at that price. The total cost for the week's expedition was £73.65 per head. This included all travel, accommodation, food, meals out, snacks and even £5.93 worth of beer.

Evening clouds on Carn Ghlusaid

Chapter 7

A Family Affair

For a number of years, Andrew had been trying to persuade Gavin Steven, one of the early Inveralligin enthusiasts, to join the annual expedition. But Gavin had moved south to work in London, had married and had two children under five, so his availability was restricted by domestic commitments. Nevertheless, he had expressed interest in the 1984 expedition, which was planned for early July in Kingussie. Somehow he had persuaded his wife, Chris, that they could travel north, rent a cottage and he could spend a few days out on the hills. To sell the idea, he persuaded Andrew that he should bring his wife, Audrey, along and that they could share accommodation, while the others could, well, do whatever they fancied. So Gavin and Andrew rented a cottage in Glen Tromie, just round the corner and up a never ending single track road from Ruthven Barracks, for a week from 23rd to 30th June. Gavin and his family travelled up overnight by Motorail from London to Inverness and on to Kingussie, to join the others. To this day Gavin's Motorail costs make his attendance the most expensive in BSSMC history, even allowing for the fact that Alastair Macrae, who worked as a mud engineer on oil rigs, often travelled from half way round the world to join the group.

Meantime, Tom had been persuading another friend from his Glasgow University days, Mike McGinnes, to join the group. Mike, who worked in the Smith Art Gallery and Museum in Stirling and lived near Stirling, was also a geologist, inevitably meaning the addition of more facial hair to the group. He drove north to meet up with Tom, Alastair and Roderick at Kingussie to form the "bachelors' group", staying at the Youth Hostel.

Sunday 24th saw the largest BSSMC group to date, six in all, assemble in Kingussie for the journey round to Creag Meagaidh. A day of low cloud and mist did not deter them from feeling their way up via "The Window", a high pass through the hills, on to the summit of Creag Meagaidh, descending to the window via a route steeper than was absolutely necessary and returning to the cars via the other Munros to the north of Coire Ardair.

While Andrew and Gavin returned to scenes of domestic chaos back at the cottage, the others enjoyed a more civilised evening meal at the hostel, followed by a quiet pint or two in the pub.

June 26th was the first birthday of Gavin's younger son, Thomas, so it was quite remarkable that Gavin had elected to join the others for a trip which would take him away from his family for a few days (he was made to pay for it later). In the run up to the annual expedition, enquiries had been made about driving in to Culra bothy to use it to access the Ben Alder hills and an energy saving itinerary had been devised. On the morning of the 25th, two cars pulled up at the row of estate workers' cottages next to the railway level crossing south of Dalwhinnie. A key was collected from a box outside the keeper's cottage, as arranged by telephone the previous week and the cars were driven over the level crossing on to an estate road to Loch Pattack. The key was for two locked gates en route, allowing a rough but manageable drive to the loch, where the cars were parked and the group completed the remaining short walk to the bothy. Having been able to complete most of the journey by car, quantities of food and fuel carried were generous, stretching even to a couple of crates of beer. The other major advantage was not having to walk too far.

Perhaps it was a feeling of guilt which forced the group into a quick ascent of Carn Dearg to the north of Culra before returning to the bothy for the evening. Thankfully, the bothy was quiet, allowing plenty room for the group to spread out and hang perishable foodstuffs in bags from nails in the walls, to protect them from the resident mice. Learning there were mice present made Alastair feel at home, having some expertise in the species. He was less happy, however, with the catering arrangements when he saw fresh vegetables, such as onions and carrots being cooked into the mince. The vegetables had been brought along only because they could be transported by car most of the way – would this mode of transport have met with the approval of the haggis eaters of 1982? Alastair elected to prepare his own mince without "bits", choosing instead to add his dried ingredients which he had been carrying in a small, cotton bag in his rucksack for years. As bothies go, Culra was fairly comfortable and allowed a reasonable night's sleep, despite Tom's best efforts to keep the others awake with his Wagnerian snoring. (It is highly likely that Tom's snoring abilities will feature in future chapters.)

Next day was one of strange weather. It was cold and windy but with a high cloud base, consisting of saucer shaped clouds which, according to the amateur weather forecasters in the group, meant a change for the worse was looming. The opportunity was taken to ascend Ben Alder by way of the long ridge, known as the "Long Leachas", a fine route with some scrambling. On reaching the summit, Alastair announced that he had made an arrangement with a friend, Ann Giles, to meet at Dalwhinnie and that if she arrived she would be joining the group for a few days. With that he rushed off on a direct descent to Loch Pattack, from where he ran down to Dalwhinnie for his rendezvous. Meanwhile the others completed a more leisurely descent via a most enjoyable traverse of Beinn Bheoil, before returning to the bothy where, in due course, Alastair arrived with his friend, Ann. After introductions, she seemed to settle in quickly to the unique, organised chaos of BSSMC life.

Unfortunately, the amateur meteorologists had been correct and the weather deteriorated overnight. Despite drizzle and low cloud a decision was taken to proceed with the ascent of the three hills west of Culra, in order to meet the objective of completing all the Munros accessible from the bothy before leaving. The ascent was made via the Lancet Edge which, according to the guide books, is a ridge of rocky outcrops narrowing to a rocky arête above steep slopes falling into Loch an Sgurr. No one seemed to notice or care as the wet weather encouraged as rapid an ascent as was possible. Route finding on the main ridge between the summits was difficult and maps and compasses were consulted frequently as minor disagreements arose regarding whose vaguely pointing finger should be followed. Further rocky scrambles were not given the attention they deserved as the group became wetter and colder, thoughts being focused firmly on reaching the final summit of Beinn Eibhinn before turning south to head for the path back to Culra. Wet clothes did not quite dry off overnight but, fortunately, nothing was planned for the next day other than the short walk to the cars at Loch Pattack and the return to Kingussie. Sadly, memories of the last day on the hills near Culra tend to be clouded by the weather and, given the remoteness of these hills, a return trip to enjoy them in better weather is a fading possibility with advancing years.

With Gavin spending the final day on a family trip to Inverness, the others spent a long day on the hills above Newtonmore via Glenballoch. At that time this round consisted of five Munros, joined by many miles of Monadhliath bog with route finding consisting of following mile after mile of rusting fence posts. A later revision of Munro's Tables reduced the total to three, with total justification, but much to the annoyance of those who had already been round them all. On the final evening the hostel group met up with the cottage group in a bistro in Kingussie, for great stovies and a few drinks, before making their varying arrangements for journeys home.

With Tom not returning to Wales until Monday of the following week, he and Andrew agreed to spend Sunday on a day trip to the Glen Lyon hills, which Andrew had been up some years before but which Tom needed to tick off in a bit of catching up – by this time they were forming the notion that they might "compleat" all the Munros together, perhaps finishing in 2000.

Around this time Andrew's cousin's son, Graham Freeland, was showing an interest in mountaineering. At the age of 17 and already a member of Strathclyde University's Mountaineering Club, Graham was developing climbing skills, but was keen to get out on to mountains more, rather than on rock faces in darkness following long evenings in pubs, which tended to be the norm in the University Club. So on Sunday 1st July 1983 Graham joined Andrew and Tom for an enjoyable round of the Glen Lyon Munros. Even at this early stage Graham's ability and enthusiasm for moving quickly on the hill was apparent, particularly on a steep descent where he left the pair of plodders far behind.

Throughout the day the conversation turned to genealogy in an effort to sort out a complicated family link which existed, not only between Andrew and Graham (2nd cousins) but between Tom and the other two. Tom's mother was related to the late wife of one of Andrew's uncles, which made Tom Andrew's umpteenth cousin by marriage and therefore Graham's even more umpteenth cousin, probably removed, by marriage – quite simple, really. Over subsequent years, Andrew and Tom have bored most BSSMC members with attempted explanations of the relationships, usually on long walks where it has been difficult for the listener to escape.

Chapter 8

Not The West Highland Way

Despite a general lack of youth in the group, there was a broad acceptance that the Youth Hostel network represented the best opportunity possible to pursue Munro bagging in "new" areas, while maintaining a reasonable level of comfort. With the notable exception of Alastair, the group definitely did not do discomfort. The hostel at Loch Lochy was particularly well located for heading off in different directions over a week, so it was chosen as the main venue for the 1985 expedition. It also retained that unique SYHA atmosphere that was gradually disappearing as hostellers demanded more and more amenities. The BSSMC didn't want comfort levels to improve too much though, lest they be considered too "soft" – a matter of balance.

Mike McGinnes joined the group again this year. He was particularly strong and fit at the time, which may have been why the schedule for the week was to be so strenuous. In fact, the 1985 expedition was to be memorable for the number of Munros climbed – 17 in the week – and more by Alastair and Tom who kept going into a second week.

The first hill of the week, climbed on the Saturday en route to Loch Lochy, was Sgurr na h'Ulaidh. The ascent was made in beautiful weather from the north west end of Glencoe. At the summit Andrew let slip that this was his 200th Munro, a proud claim which was met with derision by others in the group. But with Tom admitting that he had climbed about 190 the notion of completing the Munros was becoming a reality, with the year 2000 remaining the target for "compleation". Alastair protested at the whole idea, which he found distasteful, preferring to simply enjoy being out on and in the hills, regardless of any list in a book – a very reasonable argument, but not one which held water with Andrew and Tom, at least not until they had been up all the Munros.

Having enjoyed a warm, sunny first day, a second successive sunny day was something of a rarity, so the opportunity was seized to traverse the range of hills which appear so prominently to the west of Loch Lochy, opposite the Letterfinlay Lodge Hotel. Using two cars, the group started at "The Dark Mile" for the ascent, very quickly splitting into two groups. The fast group, comprising Alastair and Mike, followed one route while a Rutherglen Academy Former Pupils Club of Andrew, Tom and Roderick took a rather more leisurely route at a considerably more leisurely pace. The two groups finally met up on the summit of Sron a Choire Ghairbh for a late lunch, setting the pattern for the week. The views of the Great Glen, in both directions, on the descent from Meall na Teanga were particularly memorable, as was the final few hundred feet of descent through tick infested bracken. (Ticks have been a problem to several club members over the years. For a full discourse on the subject, readers should consult T. Sharpe or G. Freeland who seem to be particularly welcoming hosts).

Three dry days in succession were too much to hope for, so day three was a wet one on Gairich, up and down as quickly as possible. On the wet plod back to the cars one or two BSSMC members were secretly beginning to dismiss the whole Munro bagging idea and edging towards support for the Macrae philosophy, which generally ruled out summits in poor weather. But this shift in attitude lasted only briefly, as better weather was promised for the next day and the four tops of the Grey Corries beckoned.

Following the advice in Irvine Butterfield's "The High Mountains of Britain and Ireland", a comprehensive guidebook much used by the BSSMC over the years, the chosen route involved taking a car up a minor road from the Spean Bridge Hotel to a small farm at Coirechoille. The road was extremely rough in places but the wrecking of a car's suspension was a price worth paying for avoiding an extra couple of hundred feet of ascent. Alastair didn't start with the others. He had borrowed his sister's car for the trip and had had a minor bump. As he had to make contact with the insurance company, he drove to Fort William, having made arrangements with the others to meet them on their second summit of the day at an agreed time. Remarkably, this rendezvous worked, almost to the minute, all the more noteworthy in a time before mobile phones.

The day became increasingly hot and humid. Late in the afternoon, thunder began to threaten to the point where hair was beginning to stand on end. This threat provided the incentive to the tiring group to descend as quickly as possible on the long slog back to the cars.

With warm, sunny weather continuing there was no time to have a rest day so the group elected to climb a fairly easy outlier of the Mamores, Mullach nan Coirean, which required minimal effort. From the summit the group could see long stretches of the footpath which was rapidly becoming the badly eroded dual carriageway that is the West Highland Way. Alastair admitted to having walked it in its entirety, but from north to south, most walkers electing for the south to north route. He claimed this allowed him to meet more people as they were all coming towards him and that from his meetings he had a much better informed view of the Way and its walkers than other BSSMC members, whose opinions of the phenomenon were pretty jaundiced. Joining the Way for a few hundred yards on their way back to the cars there was heated debate about its merits. Tom had to be restrained from pulling up a signpost at one point.

The next day brought more settled weather, so the group made an early start and drove to Glen Shiel. Leaving one car at the bottom of the glen, they returned to the Cluanie Inn, the starting point for the classic walk best known as "The South Kintail Ridge", which consists of seven Munros and several other tops. As usual, the group split into a fast group, Mike and Alastair and a slow group, Andrew and Roderick. On this particular day Tom formed a sort of intermediate group on his own, having occasional contact with both the other groups. When the tail enders reached one top they could see the trailblazers on the next top. They did all meet up towards the end of the ridge for the descent to the glen, after a nine hour day which is recalled by those present as one of the most enjoyable in BSSMC history. After such a long day a decision was made to spend the night at the Cluanie Inn, with the luxury of a long soak in a bath before dinner in the bar.

At this point there is a notable and regrettable gap in BSSMC history. This was to be the only year for which no annual accounts have survived and no one knows why. Not only is there no record of expenditure, there is no record of a BSSMC annual dinner but the general consensus is that it was the meal in the Cluanie Inn.

The next day brought extremely cold, windy weather, but it was dry enough for a day on A'Ghlas-bheinn. It was difficult for some of the lighter weight members of the group to stay on their feet in the high wind. In a bit of a come-down from the previous night, the group spent the night at Ratagan Youth Hostel.

While Andrew, Rod and Mike headed home on the Saturday, Alastair and Tom had more free time and decided they would stay in the area for a few more days to enable Tom to add to his Munro tally, including the Five Sisters of Kintail and Sgurr Ruadh, which Andrew had climbed already. The pair chose to stay at a private hostel near Achnasheen, a less than salubrious establishment. Had it not been for the presence of two young women, Heather and Lesley, whom they felt obliged to protect from the less pleasant aspects of life in the hostel, they may have chosen not to stay there at all – how chivalrous! In the evening, Alastair and Tom were persuaded by the hostel proprietor to give him a lift to the Achnasheen Hotel where he wanted to play pool. At that time Tom played pool reasonably well and made the mistake of upsetting his host by beating him. The unpleasantness which followed resulted in the bad loser being left to make his own way back to his hostel, rather the worse for drink. What followed is best not recorded but their stay at the hostel became the next BSSMC legend.

The by now rampant Munro bagging duo (Alastair objecting strongly to this description) continued with an ascent of Gleouraich before heading for Glencoe and a rapid traverse of the Aonach Eagach which saw them back in the Clachaig Inn for lunch – how fitness standards have fallen since those heady days.

Chapter 9

The Happy Wanderers

Seeking access to hills from the highest possible altitude, some BSSMC members were attracted to Glenshee and the Devil's Elbow as an area of considerable potential for the 1986 expedition. Of course, life could never be as simple as ascending all the week's Munros from the top station of a chairlift, so there was a bit more to the week than that initial attractive prospect. This was to be another unadulterated Munro-bagging expedition, the idea being – maximum Munros, minimum effort, but this was to backfire at least once during the week.

Shunning the relative luxuries of the Youth Hostel at Braemar, the more spartan hostel at Inverey was selected as the starting venue. With no running water, outside toilets and gas lighting, it provided an acceptable notion of "roughing it". Records show that in 1986 this standard of hostel accommodation cost £2.20 per adult per night.

The week began on 28th June using two cars for the ascent of four Munros to the east of Glenshee, the day soured only by the annihilation of a family of oyster catchers, mowed down by Roderick who, quite correctly, chose the option of genocide over putting his passengers at risk by swerving to avoid this mis-timed family outing of maw, paw and baby oyster catchers on the A93.

Despite protests by Alastair, the chairlift was used next day to whisk the group to the summit of The Cairnwell. While Alastair thought the process unethical, his protest did not extend to making a lone ascent on foot. After an easy start, the round of four Munros west of the Devil's Elbow was completed with relative ease. The chairlift may have provided an easy start to the day, but the end to the day more than made up for it. After dinner, the group packed rucksacks for a late evening walk into the Lairig Ghru from Linn O'Dee, intending to stay overnight at Corrour Bothy. Whether the filthy state of the bothy (sadly a common occurrence), the presence of other occupants or simply the beautiful evening caused a change of plan is unclear, but Andrew, Roderick and Tom elected to bivouac high in the corrie above the bothy, while Alastair and Mike stuck with the original plan – missing a wonderful experience. It was a beautiful night; dry, bright and sunny until after 11pm. The sun rose again at around 4am, casting pink, shadowy light round the corrie. Those who had slept enjoyed a magnificent sunrise. Those who hadn't slept simply enjoyed being able to get out of their sleeping bags for breakfast.

The day began with the earliest start in BSSMC history. By what would normally be considered breakfast time, the group was standing on top of the Devil's Point. As the sun rose higher and the temperature increased they made their way over Cairn Toul, Beinn Bhrotain and Monadh Mor, making the conscious decision to contour round the summit of Sgorr an Lochain Uaine which, at that time, was not designated a Munro and was simply, therefore, considered by some as an un-necessary expenditure of energy. On several occasions, fights almost broke out as members of the group tried to secure any available square inch or two of shade, behind a trig point or cairn for example. With the temperature soaring and the effects of the previous day's efforts beginning to be noticed, the long walk back to Linn O'Dee seemed never ending. At one point Roderick simply keeled over, fortunately into a soft landing in heathery peat, suffering from severe heat stroke and dehydration.

Back at the hostel next day, some tasks which seemed un-necessarily strenuous were being allocated by the temporary warden, a young French girl, who took more than a passing interest in the group's cooking. Observing breakfast being prepared, she asked,

"Ees zis zee famous scrumeled egg, no?"

"Zis ees zee famous scrumeled egg, yes," was the reply.

"Would you like to try some?" she was asked, out of politeness.

"No thanks", she replied, turning up her nose – unimpressed by zee scrumeled egg.

Her response was met with a collective sigh of relief from the diners who would not have been happy had their rations been reduced. After some clearing of a drain and toilet cleaning, under mademoiselle's watchful eye, the rest of the day was declared an official day of rest, to allow recovery from the efforts of the previous two days.

A trip over the Lecht to Tomintoul and Grantown On Spey for lunch was followed by a return visit to the Macallan Distillery which, once again, was officially closed for the summer holiday and annual maintenance. On this occasion the manager gave the group a brief tour, culminating in a visit to the "secret room" in Easter Elchies House, where a generous dram was poured and entertainment was provided in the form of a multi-media presentation which included music from a magnificent fairground organ. The organ, in what is actually the music room of the house, is still in working order but is no longer accessible to the public.

A further hot day on the Wednesday provided ideal conditions for a return trip over the Devil's Elbow to leave cars at the Coiremulzie Hotel at Spittal of Glenshee. The walk in to Glas Tulaichan saw the group walking in close order for a change, almost marching in step. Conversation turned to marching songs suitable for such an occasion and it seemed to the group that German walkers would be the most likely nationality to have songs for such circumstances. "The Happy Wanderer" seemed like the ideal song, but with German words. As no-one in the group spoke German, words were made up. As confidence in their home made German increased, so did the volume as chorus after chorus rang out. Little thought was given to any fellow walkers on the hill that day who may have been hoping for a quiet day out. The noisy chorus was halted by the sighting of a black bird with a white mark on its chest. There followed a half hour debate on bird identification – not a strong subject in the group – until it was finally concluded that it was definitely not a dipper but may have been a ring ouzel. Any living object and certainly anything younger than about ten million years of age held little interest for sixty percent of the group (the geologists).

Further verses of the Happy Wanderer faded as the slopes of Glas Tulaichan steepened. Two more Munros were ticked off on what was becoming a long day. Further musical interludes followed, when down slopes permitted breath to be drawn. The theme to the children's television cartoon, Captain Pugwash, seemed to be another group favourite. It didn't have any words, which helped. It went, "deedle ee dee deedle ee dee, dum de dum da dee dee dee dee," and repeat. Over subsequent years it became a sort of BSSMC theme tune.

Thursday was hot and humid, although visibility was poor. An "easy" hill accessed by a track almost opposite the hostel, Carn Bhac, was the final un-climbed hill in the immediate vicinity, so it was selected for the day's effort. It would have been much easier had Tom's knee not given up the ghost a few hundred feet below the summit. He was determined to make it to the top, very slowly, but getting back down was to prove a real problem. Andrew and Mike tried various forms of assistance, four handed seats, arms over shoulders etc, but Tom's weight proved too much for any sustained level of support. Once down on the track, two country gents in a Landrover spotted the struggling Tom and gave him a lift back to the hostel. The others walked back. That night the group drove to Kingussie, checked in to the Youth Hostel, then ate out at a total cost of £20 apparently.

Although the weather was hot and sunny on the Friday, everyone agreed that another day of rest was required so the opportunity was taken to visit the bright lights of Aviemore. Here, a new activity was introduced into the BSSMC agenda – putting. The annual accounts record that Mike won this inaugural putting competition and there was a declared intention that this should become an annual event, a good excuse for a day off from the hills. There was also an indulgent lunch of pizza, total cost £18.

It was back out on to the hills, or hill to be precise, on the Saturday – the extremely uninteresting Geal Charn (there are four Munros bearing this common name and they are all pretty uninteresting) above Glen Markie, near Laggan. Another one "ticked off."

Andrew and Roderick then returned home while the others spent a further night at the hostel and climbed Stuchd an Lochain on Sunday on their way home. The week had been marked by the distinct lack of rain, a rare occurrence.

Chapter 10

Moniack Munros

As had become the norm, the venue for the annual expedition had been agreed, in broad terms, at the close of the previous year's meet. The area near Beauly had been selected, offering access to Ben Wyvis and a number of hills along the road to Achnashellach.

Over the winter, Andrew had been recruiting a new member. Graham Freeland, who had joined Tom and Andrew in 1984 for a day in Glen Lyon, had continued to develop his interest in walking and climbing and had expressed interest in joining the group, despite its increasingly geriatric nature. There remains some suspicion that there was an ulterior motive for encouraging Graham's interest in joining – the identified need to have a competent climber to lead the assault on Skye, an inevitable project if "compleation" was ever to be a reality.

With the likelihood of six participants in the 1987 expedition, a cottage in Cabrich near Beauly had been rented. It was a newly converted crofthouse owned by a retired Glasgow policeman who had gone into the holiday rental business courtesy of the demise of a number of aged relatives who had owned crofts in the area. This was to be his first let and, on hearing that his first tenants would be an all male group, he had been slightly hesitant in agreeing the let but he had been assured that the group consisted of middle aged, housetrained gentlemen, whose healthy life style would take them well away from the cottage most days and that in the evenings they would be too tired to even consider engaging in any form of remotely boisterous behaviour.

On Saturday 27th June three cars pulled up outside the cottage to be met by the aforementioned "Bobby", who remained apprehensive about his first let, particularly as he seemed to have forgotten that the group would be all male. Mike's bushy hair and beard and Graham's youthful exuberance did nothing to quell his anxiety. Even Roderick's respectable appearance carried no weight. As they unpacked the cars, Andrew, tried to reassure "Bobby" with talk of the group's healthy lifestyle. Meanwhile Graham, clearly keen to impress his new companions by his willingness to do his bit, was enthusiastically unloading several crates of McEwan's Export and a couple of bottles of whisky from the boot – not the image Andrew was trying to portray. However, "Bobby" was successfully distracted and he was finally placated. A very comfortable base camp was established, at a cost of £120 for the week. Incidentally, "Bobby" visited the group several times during the week and seemed quite happy.

The week began well with a pleasant day on two outlying hills near the Fannichs, followed by another good day on two mountains south of Craig, near Achnashellach and an uneventful day on Ben Wyvis. Then followed the major mountaineering exploit of the week, a round of the Fannichs, accessed from the south with permission having been obtained to take a car in part of the way. The group was joined for the day by Cathy Niven and her husband, Roger. Cathy, by her own admission, was not very fit and Tom's Achilles Heel, better known as his knee, was causing him great pain from early in the day, so it was not long before the group split. One group of Tom, Roderick, Cathy and Roger opted for a relatively leisurely day, taking in only a couple of summits, while the other group of Andrew, Graham and Mike completed a round of 7 Munros in 10½ hours. During the latter stages of this round Andrew was to witness Graham's blistering pace on the hill, as he watched Mike and Graham pull away in front of him, accelerating each time they hit an uphill stretch. Eventually Mike, no slouch himself, was left behind as he struggled to stay in Graham's slipstream. Over subsequent years, Graham's walking speed on the hills went on to become something of first wonder and amazement, then jealousy and finally frustration at their own inadequacies, to other members of the group or, to be more precise, to Andrew and Tom, as Mike and Alastair could give him a run, literally, for his money some of the time.

Having mentioned Alastair, reference should be made to his arrival, on the Thursday morning. His work schedule and travel arrangements meant he had had to make the journey from Glasgow by train overnight, arriving at Beauly station at 6.30am. As Andrew arrived at the station to meet him he was already well into a can of McEwan's Export as he sat at a picnic table. He explained that, having been travelling for several days, it was not 6.30am according to his body clock. He was very wide awake, having been entertained by a fellow traveller who thought he was on a local service from Glasgow to Cathcart and was surprised, as he shared a beer and conversation with Alastair, to find the train approaching Larbert, where the guard arranged to let him off.

A fairly easy day, well really a fairly easy 4 hours, followed for Alastair, Tom and Andrew on Fionn Bheinn (one to remember for one's old age). Records show that the others didn't join them. This left time for an afternoon visit to the nearby Moniack Winery where, after a brief conducted tour the whole group indulged, some would say over-indulged, in a wine tasting session on a generous scale. The proprietor's generosity, however, was rewarded by a group order which, according to accounts, cost £79.62. It was fortunate that the cottage was close by.

The following day the group was joined by Malcolm Smith, a work colleague of Andrew's, who lived in nearby Kiltarlity. Malcolm was an enthusiastic ornithologist who spent much of his leisure time recording and counting various bird species for the RSPB. As they walked in to climb Tom a' Choinnich and Toll Creagach, his knowledge of local bird life and stories of his long trips into some of the remotest parts of the country made Munro Bagging seem like a pretty pathetic activity, but not for long. One may wonder if Malcolm ever bumped into Jimmy Jamieson – they seemed to frequent similar wilderness areas.

The annual dinner was held in the Kiltarlity Hotel, the total bill, excluding drinks, was £45. It was during this dinner that Graham introduced a whole range of alcoholic drinks to his older friends, about which they knew nothing and whose names they could barely pronounce. Heads shook at the ridiculous drinking habits of young folk, as Graham's elders supped their delicious pints of McEwan's Export and the like. Incidentally, in a group where everyone took it in turn to pay a group cost of one sort of another, with expenditure being recorded and a reckoning carried out on the final day, it appears that Graham contributed 50 pence, for the electric meter. The total cost per person for the week, covering accommodation, transport and food, was £70.41. Graham did, of course, settle his account – eventually.

On the return journey home, Mike, Roderick and Tom "climbed" Creise in Glencoe, with the help of the chairlift, to help Tom plug a Munro gap. It is not clear why the others didn't join them.

This had been a very successful week, with new blood helping raise Andrew and Tom's adrenalin levels as their thoughts began to turn to Skye and the Inaccessible Pinnacle – but not just yet.

Lochan na h-Earba

The Devil's Ridge

Climbing the Inaccessible Pinnacle

Graham abseiling from the Inaccessible Pinnacle

The Shelter Stone, Cairngorms

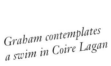

*Graham contemplates
a swim in Coire Lagan*

The Inaccessible Pinnacle from Coireachan Ruadha

Alastair on Sgurr Thuilm

The Summit Ridge of Bidein a Choire Sheasgaich

Chapter 11

The Christening

After having decided they were still not quite ready to tackle the challenge of Skye (would they ever be?), the group elected for another west coast venue in 1988. Travelling from Cardiff, Manchester, Peebles, Glasgow, Stirling and in Alastair's case from somewhere close to the back of beyond, a six strong group met on Saturday 18th June in Tyndrum for coffee. The venue was the Clifton Coffee House and Craft Centre, which had been a meeting place for members of the group for many years, dating back to day trips from Rutherglen. BSSMC members have watched its development and growth over a long number of years, partly attributable, no doubt, to the number of coffees, scones and other goodies they have purchased there.

The present business started in 1965 as "Gosden of Tyndrum", then only a Post Office, general store and a single petrol pump. The first small coffee shop on the premises opened in 1967, before further expansion saw it become "The Clifton Coffee House and Craft Centre". After further development the adjacent "Green Welly Shop" opened in 1980. Finally it became a much bigger enterprise, "The Green Welly Stop", the extremely busy rest stop familiar to so many tourists travelling north to Oban or Glencoe.

A combination of good weather and start of the week enthusiasm led to an afternoon ascent of Beinn Sgulaird from the head of Loch Creran. It was therefore late afternoon before they continued on to their final destination, a privately operated bunkhouse near Onich, in which accommodation had been booked in advance. Although fairly new, the bunkhouse was not the best maintained establishment the group had ever visited. The main room had an Alpine hut style sleeping platform along one wall and a dining area occupying the remainder of the room. A small kitchen offered completely inadequate cooking facilities for the numbers the place could accommodate and washing and toilet facilities were rather overcrowded too. Fortunately there were a couple of showers which helped keep things civilised. There was also a small dormitory off the main room. It had three bunk beds and offered some privacy. The group of six was pleased to be allocated this room to which they were given a key, enabling belongings to be left safely while they were out.

The bunkhouse was busy. For much of the week, two other groups were present, in addition to the odd person or two passing through. There was a group of Boy Scouts, apparently there to do some hill walking, and a very organised, mixed gender group following a vegetarian diet, who spent each evening pouring over maps and discussing the next day's route in great detail. The Boy Scouts spent most of their evenings in some very giggly under aged drinking in the public bar of a nearby hotel, having abandoned half eaten meals, possibly in their haste to get to the pub or possibly because the food was of the variety which only Boy Scouts and BB boys eat. On their return from the pub, they continued to giggle as others tried to sleep, then in the morning they lay on in their sleeping bags as others cooked breakfast and prepared to leave for the hills. The Boy Scouts were apparently not impressed by the planning, organisation or mountaineering stamina of the two older groups.

With Munros in every direction, the reason Onich had been chosen in the first place, it was to be a busy week. On the Sunday the group drove round to Tulloch near Roy Bridge for a day on two Munros followed on Monday by a return trip down the south side of Loch Linnhe to the head of Loch Creran, for an ascent of Beinn Fhionnlaidh this time, the weather remaining hot and sultry.

Over the years most of the group had been up most of the Mamores, but not necessarily the same summits. In addition this was a range which was constantly subject to height revision and therefore changes in Munro status, in successive editions of Munro's Tables, so the opportunity was taken to have a couple of days in the area. The first trip was devoted to the outlying summit of Sgurr Eilde Mor. To shorten the day, cars were taken to a remote hotel, high above the north shore of Loch Leven. The hotel was run down, damp smelling and strangely deserted. But as the group drank morning coffee, which was more chicory than coffee, in a damp and dusty lounge, where the loud tick of an old grandfather clock seemed deafening in the otherwise silent hotel, they became increasingly aware of a number of elderly guests, or residents, sleeping in chairs or wandering aimlessly along grey corridors, blank looks on their faces. Was this really a hotel or had it been converted to an out of the way home for the elderly from where they could be despatched to the great mountain home in the sky with minimal attention? Having paid to leave cars there for the day, the group was glad to leave this place behind and set off into the comforting moist cloud which prevailed for much of the day.

Next day, Andrew, Graham and Tom drove out to Loch Quoich to climb Sgurr a' Mhaoraich before the whole group re-assembled for a long day on the middle section of the Mamore range, starting and finishing at the head of Glen Nevis and taking in the tops between An Gearanach and Stob Ban with the added interest of the Devil's Ridge, an entertaining scramble, in dull, warm but mainly dry weather.

On a roll of decent weather, a return trip to the Laggan area followed for a sunny day out on two summits to the south of Loch Laggan. The route took the group past the beautiful, small, sandy beach at the south west end of Lochan na h-Earba, offering lovely views up the loch towards the area used some years later as the setting for the BBC series "Monarch of the Glen." This is one of these places which is only a short walk from a main road and sticks in the mind as a place worth walking to as a destination in its own right when legs no longer support uphill travel.

Given the limitations of the cooking facilities back at the bunkhouse, it is perhaps not surprising that the group ate out twice during the week, although neither meal seems to have been designated the official dinner. What is recorded is that one of the meals was in the Spean Bridge Hotel and seems to have been a pretty fishy affair, with orders including herring, mackerel and salmon quiche. The second, on the final night, was in the newly opened restaurant near the bunkhouse. While Graham ate prawn cocktail, followed by scampi, Tom had soup, followed by sirloin steak. These menu selections became fairly predictable through the late 1980s and 1990s.

After a very full and successful week the group prepared to leave the bunkhouse on Saturday 25th June. They opened the bunkhouse log book to record the week's exploits to find that the Boy Scouts had been there first. With remarkable eloquence, wit and extensive vocabulary, they had described not so much their own activities, but had recorded their thoughts on the other groups in the bunkhouse. The vegetarian route planners were entitled "The Beans and Lentils Bumbles and Stumbles Brigade", while the other group of six mature, intelligent, active males was described as a secretive group, apparently from one of the more posh areas near Glasgow, whose members didn't mix with anyone else, who locked themselves and their belongings in their own private room, went to bed early and spent all day on mountains. The Scouts had christened this group "The Bearsden Secret Society Mountaineering Club."

Initially taken aback by the cheeky description, the members of the group gradually warmed to the title. No one came from, had ever lived in, or had any connection with Bearsden. They had never thought of themselves as a club and membership numbers could barely justify that description, but mountaineering was what they were trying to do while the idea of mystery, suggested by being a secret society, was quite appealing. When it became apparent that, if abbreviated to BSSMC the title had vague overtones of Scottish Mountaineering Club about it, it was agreed that this would be the name of the "club" from that time forth.

So, on Saturday 25th June 1988, the newly christened BSSMC left Onich, deciding to have its first official outing as a club to Ben Chonzie. The ascent was made from Glen Lednock near Comrie before the group split up to head off on their various journeys home. No one went to Bearsden.

Chapter 12

Sutherland

As Andrew and Tom marched slowly but surely towards "compleation", the more they began to appreciate the complexity of the task ahead. There were several distinct areas they had not visited, like Skye, there were remote hills which could not easily be visited in a single day, both had climbed hills the other hadn't, there were odd gaps where tops had been missed on earlier visits, perhaps due to bad weather and there was, of course, the periodic revision of Munro's Tables to complicate matters.

One such problem was Sutherland. Although there were only four Munros in the whole of Caithness and Sutherland, they were a long way away from home bases and were rather too spread out for easy access, at least in terms of the customary week's annual outing. So, considerable planning went into the trip north in the last week of June 1989 for the BSSMC group of Andrew, Graham, Mike, Roderick and Tom. The plan was to use Youth Hostels at Tongue, Ullapool and Carbisdale and to hope for good weather. It is, uninterestingly, on record that the week's rations were purchased in William Low's and Presto, perhaps illustrating the BSSMC's lack of loyalty to any single supermarket chain.

After a long drive north, the group stayed at Tongue Y.H for the first two nights, climbing Ben Hope, the most northerly of the Munros, on 25th June. The hostel was a large, stone built, traditional highland villa on the outskirts of the village, sparsely furnished but clean and there was a good pub in the nearby hotel. The annual accounts for this year are rather sketchy, but it would appear that eating at the pub was the preferred option. Next day, the group drove south to Ben Klibreck, a pleasant enough hill but not particularly memorable, before driving on to the magnificent hostel in Carbisdale Castle, which had been pre booked.

Carbisdale Castle Hostel is unique and possibly one of the most magnificent youth hostels in the world. A long rhododendron lined drive leads to a large gravel car park in front of the castle, which was built originally for the Dowager Duchess of Sutherland, a lady with a very colourful history, between 1906 and 1917 before being bequeathed to the SYHA in 1945. Inside, the main hall is lined with suits of armour, Italian marble statues and large landscape and portrait paintings. The grand staircase leads to a network of corridors with dormitories and toilets off. One could easily get lost in this place and bump into the resident ghost.

With a timetable to follow, Carbisdale was left behind with some regret as the group drove to Ullapool on the 27th. It was raining when they arrived and it continued to rain for most of the day but, having spent as much time as feasible exploring the delights of Ullapool, the group ate early and as the rain began to ease during the evening, they made a very late rush up Eididh nan Clach Geala, leaving cars in Gleann na Sguaib under Roderick's watchful eye. They returned to the cars in semi darkness, just as Roderick was beginning to become slightly concerned, and made it back to the hostel before locking up time, to some strange looks from fellow hostellers. Ullapool YH is a complete contrast to Carbisdale. It is a compact hostel with bustling communal rooms and is always lively. Its location on the shore not far from the pier provides a magnificent panorama out over the loch and east to the hills of the Beinn Dearg group.

Ullapool hostel was home for three nights, coinciding with some very wet weather. Having already spent half of a wet day in Ullapool, more than enough for even the most patient soul, the group was prepared to go along with Tom's suggestion that they should visit the famous caves at Inchnadamph the next day. During the 1980s Tom had developed an interest in caving, an activity he assured the others was really enjoyable and quite safe if one took appropriate precautions and carried proper equipment. Suitably reassured, they arrived at Cnoc na Uamh in very damp weather and eventually located the entrance to the cave network. Led by Tom like lambs to the slaughter, they entered the cave armed with a rope and torches (proper equipment!!). While it was very interesting to experience total darkness, all apart from Tom concluded that confined spaces in darkness, with an unknown depth of running water at their feet, were not to be recommended. The brief visit was soon abandoned, although Tom and Graham ventured a short distance further into the cave. Tom, however, maintained an unhealthy interest in caving, including caves in which it was necessary to spend a deal of time in and under water. Surely, only masochists can possibly enjoy this activity but it is deemed necessary to describe it in more detail to deter any reader who may be thinking about giving it a try.

Imagine a narrow tunnel which is high enough to crawl through only if one's head is turned to one side and one's feet are similarly splayed. One wriggles like a centipede until a sump (like a small bath) full of water, is encountered. One takes a deep breath and propels one's body forward, completely immersed in cold, dirty water, arching one's back under a large rock which is sticking down into the water, hoping that a space containing air will appear at the other end of the water filled sump before one needs to breath again. The person who has gone in front may help by pulling one's head out of the water. Cold and wet, running the risk of having contracted Weil's Disease from swallowing water contaminated by rat urine, one then makes one's way along passages so narrow that exhaling fully is the only method of squeezing through, into chambers containing water which may rise at any time if it rains heavily outside. Assuming one has survived so far one has to face the return journey, either by the same route in reverse or by another, equally uncomfortable series of tortures. No?

It was wet again on the 29th but the group elected to set off for Am Faochagach, attempting an ascent up a long spur just north of the dam on Loch Glascarnoch. In dry conditions this would have been a tiresome plod through deep heather. After several days of rain and in ongoing precipitation it was awful. At some point there was general agreement that the attempt should be abandoned and a retreat was made to Ullapool, where the local attractions hadn't improved significantly over the past few days.

The weather on 30th June was marginally better, but still damp. Being their last day, the group decided to climb Ben More Assynt and Conival to complete the week. In good weather, this would have been a great day out and, as it was, the ridge between the two summits was most enjoyable, but the long, damp trek back through very wet bog was a disappointing way to finish the week.

There was an annual dinner on the final evening, but the venue is not recorded. The total cost of £24.45 for five suggests it cannot have been particularly memorable. Graham probably had scampi.

Chapter 13

The World Cup Final Expedition

Blair Atholl was the venue for the 1990 annual expedition and a static caravan on the very well run site next to Blair Castle had been booked, giving a good base for the hills round Glen Tilt and the A9. The caravan was well equipped, if rather cramped, for 5 occupants (Andrew, Graham, Mike, Rod and Tom) who were well able to spread out to exceed the space available, particularly if clothes needed to be dried. At a cost of £180 for the week it was, however, a good deal.

The first week in July began well with a cloudy but dry day on Beinn Dearg followed by an easy day in Glen Tilt to climb Carn a'Chlamain by a very good stalker's path. Permission had been obtained from Blair Castle Estate office to take a car up Glen Tilt as far as Forest Lodge, making life easier, an option no longer available to today's Munro baggers. While the hill itself was not particularly memorable, Tom's recollections are of a visit to one of the most significant locations in the history of geology. James Hutton, the famous Edinburgh geologist and father of modern geology visited Glen Tilt in the 1780s (really modern!) in search of evidence to prove that certain rocks originated as a molten mass, contrary to the belief of many geologists of the time, particularly those of the German mining academy at Freiburg where the pupils of Abraham Gottlob Werner supported the idea that all rocks originated under water. This was the famous scientific battle between the Neptunists and the Vulcanists (nothing to do with Mr Spock). Hutton's visit to Glen Tilt was in search of the contact between the schist rock of the Central Highlands and the granite masses which he knew lay to the north. Near Forest Lodge, Hutton saw veins of granite interfingering with the schists which could only have come about had the granite once been molten and been injected into the schists. Illustrations of Forest Lodge and the rocks nearby were prepared by a friend of Hutton's in the 1780s and the site can be recognised easily today from these illustrations. This is one of the classic sites in world geology – not a lot of people know that!

Andrew had to return home to attend a funeral, so the others took the opportunity to travel across to Spean Bridge to visit Aonach Mor and Aonach Beag, hills Andrew had climbed many years before and was happy to miss, but Tom still needed to tick them off on his list. This BSSMC visit coincided with the recent opening of the gondola on Aonach Mor, which they felt obliged to try out of course, at a cost to the group of £14.80. Tom insisted it was of little real assistance as it doesn't go very far up the hill.

Andrew rejoined the group that evening but, having had three consecutive days on the hill, the rest of the group declared 4th July as a rest day. It began with a trip to Pitlochry for the BSSMC putting competition. Pitlochry's putting green was and is a wonderfully challenging course, built into a steep hill, with most holes including slopes of varying steepness and direction. Real golfers find it challenging and tend to take it very seriously while non-golfers simply have a laugh at the 28 strokes needed for some holes. Of the five non-golfing BSSMC members, Andrew's luck held and he emerged victorious (he didn't admit to the others that he had played the course several times before). The accounts for the week show that after the putting competition a round of ice creams cost £2.70.

Travelling from Pitlochry to the Macallan distillery may not seem an obvious side trip but that is what the BSSMC did later that day. From previous visits they would have known that production would have been closed down for the summer holiday but they were confident that some form of hospitality would still be on offer – what a distance to travel for a free dram!

On arrival the distillery manager was aware that some of the group had visited before and scratched his head to think of something novel to show them. "Have you ever been in the lab?" he asked. They hadn't so, as the "chemist" was working in the lab that day they were invited in. It reminded them of a school science lab with labelled flasks of amber liquid on shelves, test tubes, flasks and a man in a white lab coat. The "chemist" politely answered a series of questions about the distilling and maturing process and spoke knowledgably about "nosing" whisky. He was asked about the oldest whisky he had nosed.

"Sixty four" he replied.

"From 1964?"

"No, 64 years old. I think I might have some here."

A dusty flask was pulled off a shelf and he poured some of the quite dark gold liquid into a nosing glass and, turning his back on the group to resume his work, encouraged the group to "nose it", which they did. On handing the glass back, the "chemist" expressed slight surprise that the group hadn't drunk any of the whisky. The group response was that they had assumed they had been invited to "nose" rather than taste. He nodded and proceeded to empty the glass down the sink. Hearing a gasp he shrugged and explained,

"Now that it's been near your noses I can't put it back – it's no use now. By the way, you might be interested to know that a bottle of this sold recently for £7000. What did you think of it?"

There was agreement that it smelled more like sherry than whisky but that the overwhelming smell was one of wood. He nodded.

"After 64 years in an oak sherry cask, wood is about all you get. But I doubt if anyone will ever drink it anyway, it's just been bought by a collector as an investment." This was an opinion they had heard before in that distillery.

Still a bit shocked at having watched a £300 dram washed down the sink, the group made the long trip back to Pitlochry. Incidentally, Andrew came across the £7000 bottle a year later, in a roadside inn south of Oban, on display in a glass case. The owner was rather taken aback when he heard that Andrew had actually "nosed" his whisky but confirmed that he had indeed bought it as an investment and had no intention of drinking it.

Next day the full group made the long drive out to the north west end of Glen Lyon to ascend a hill (Meall Buidhe) which, were it not for its Munro status, would attract little attention. It was the sort of day which gave lots of opportunities for Tom to indulge in one of his favourite pursuits, visiting remote little tea rooms for coffee and scones. This was followed by a very warm but hazy day on Beinn A'Ghlo, which has three Munros, each one progressively further away from the starting point and therefore necessitating a long walk back at the end of the day. It is probably the long walk back which lingers in the mind and dulls the sense of enjoyment of this particular group of hills.

The 1990 expedition coincided with the later stages of the finals of the football World Cup in Italy. However, as usual, Scotland had been eliminated at the first group stage while England had progressed, so none of the group had any real interest in the later stages of the tournament. The group would normally have tended to drift towards one or other of the local hotels in the evenings, but the public bar in one was not particularly tourist friendly and the lounge in the other was, well, just too touristy, so football crept back into the evening entertainment schedule as the tournament progressed. Armed with a substantial carry-out in the caravan, the BSSMC threw its collective support behind the mighty Cameroon, as they came up against those World Cup minnows, England on 1st July. Against all expectations, Cameroon took the lead early in the second half. A huge roar emanated from the BSSMC caravan, which rocked in celebration, to the extent that the wall mural of used beer cans fell to the floor, much to the consternation and disgust of neighbouring English caravaners. Despite a valiant effort by Cameroon, England finally triumphed in extra time through a penalty, resulting in a few more cans being emptied in commiseration before being added to the re-erected mural. The BSSMC supporters club was, however, rather fickle. No sooner had their team been defeated than they were supporting Germany, who happened to be playing England on 4th July. There was a further evening of rocking and rolling in the caravan as Germany emerged victorious. Signs of disgust from neighbours became even more apparent.

The annual dinner on Friday 6th July was held in the very tartan lounge bar of the Atholl Arms Hotel but, other than its total cost of £40, there is no record of it – it was probably one of those typical Highland bar meals which sounds better from the description on the menu than it actually tastes, but scampi probably featured.

Chapter 14

Skye in the Rain

By 1991, Graham's rock climbing skills had become sufficiently rusty that, when the BSSMC announced that this was to be the year for a visit to Skye, he spent much of the spring revising how to tie a figure of eight and other knots. However, his knowledge and experience on rock was way beyond anything Andrew or Tom could offer and they had complete faith he would be able to pull them up anything they might encounter on Skye. Considerable thought had gone into deciding that early June offered the best chance of dry, possibly even sunny weather - and possibly midge free too. A cottage at Sligachan was identified as an ideal base and a booking was made, the cost being £200 for the week. So, on 8th June, armed with a couple of ropes and some hardware supplied by Graham, a 5 strong BSSMC expedition set off, over the sea to Skye (the ferry from Kyle of Lochalsh to Kyleakin was the main route in those bygone pre-bridge days). In a change of personnel, Alastair had replaced Mike.

There was an air of excited anticipation as the group drove off the ferry and on to Sligachan. Group optimism took its first knock on the drive north as a light drizzle appeared, gradually developing into constant, heavy rain as they arrived at the cottage. Standing outside the cottage, waiting for someone to arrive with a key, they couldn't help notice that the midges had made an early appearance this year. However, the cottage was ideal. A loft with a drop down ladder provided sufficient vertical space for a makeshift abseil practice area and climbing hardware classroom. It had the usual living amenities too.

Despite the continuing drizzle and low cloud next day, the group made a determined assault on Blaven. None of the participants would be able to describe anything of the mountain, other than it having some very steep rocky bits, as the thick mist and cloud restricted views to a few feet of the tourist route in front of them. The weather prevented further exploration of this fine hill and they had to content themselves with having reached the summit and returning safely.

The next couple of days were spent looking out of the cottage window at what should have been a fine view of Sgurr nan Gillean but which was instead a fuzzy grey blur, the only visible movement being a constant cloud of hovering midges, eagerly awaiting anyone stupid enough to open the door. There was a limit to the amount of time the group could tolerate sampling the delights of Portree, so a decision was made to head for Coire Lagan.

The walk into the corrie was extremely wet underfoot, overhead and everywhere in between. Discarding the use of map and compass, which they knew to be particularly unreliable in Skye due to the magnetic nature of the rock, they found themselves on some huge gabbro slabs. Alastair assured the others that he had been there before and recognised this as a route into the corrie. As they climbed higher they became wetter and colder and increasingly disorientated. They were therefore in no fit state to remember that Alastair's routes often led to places Alastair wanted to go rather than to a named location. Attempts to establish their location involved techniques such as wind direction and detailed geological assessments of rock features. Eventually, with hypothermia threatening, there was reluctant acceptance that they hadn't a clue where they were. It was Tom's skill (or so he claims) in recognising the direction of the glacial striae which indicated the direction into the corrie. These (the striae) were followed and the corrie lochan appeared through the mist. Having relocated themselves in time and space, the path was soon located and a hasty retreat was made through the boggy path leading back to the cars in Glenbrittle. Portree didn't seem so bad after that.

The following poem, written by that prolific poet "Anonymous" describes the prevailing weather rather well.

It rained and rained, rained and rained,
The average fall was well maintained
And when the tracks were simple bogs
It started raining cats and dogs.
After a drought of half an hour
We had a most refreshing shower
And the most amazing thing of all -
Gentle rain began to fall.
Next day but one was fairly dry
Save for one deluge from the sky
Which wetted the party to the skin
Until at last the rain set in.

June 13th didn't produce a view of Sgurr nan Gillean, but it was possible to see the water running off the hill from the cottage window so, taking the improved visibility as a sign that the rain was easing, the group set off across a very boggy bog from where Andrew, Graham and Tom completed the ascent of Sgurr nan Gillean. No view, wet, cold, but ticked off – what a sad approach to mountaineering.

June 14th was marginally better. The low cloud prevailed but it was more or less dry. With so much preparation having been carried out, this had to be the day for the Inaccessible Pinnacle, so the 5 strong group made a fairly quick ascent of Sgurr Dearg, from where some serious contemplation of the Pinnacle itself, through swirling mist, took place – for about an hour. After a brief attempt by Graham to scale the short side of the Pinnacle it was abundantly clear that it would be beyond the capabilities of the others, so attention turned to the longer but technically easier route. The start of the route was fairly obvious and the group set off, apart from Roderick, who watched from a safe distance. Alastair turned back fairly quickly, not convinced that the others knew what they were doing or that conditions were suitable for such a serious endeavour. Graham was, however, "encouraged" by Andrew and Tom to lead on, roped to nothing in particular. As Graham disappeared out of sight he knew he was off route, hopelessly exposed, with the rope of little use to him in the event of a fall. Whether he took time to change his underwear on his return to the proper route on the crest of the ridge is not recorded, but as he brought Andrew and Tom up to join him he displayed sufficient composure to let them believe everything was under control. The final push to the summit, up an extremely narrow crest but with good holds, was fairly straightforward, the mist concealing the ridiculous exposure of the place. They reached the small platform of the summit of the Pinnacle but contained their celebrations until all three had abseiled safely down to rejoin Roderick and Alastair. Feelings were very mixed. Roderick was pleased to see the others again, having wondered if he ever would. Alastair was angry that Andrew and Tom had pushed Graham into an unreasonably unsafe situation. Graham was very relieved to be on firm ground after his not totally voluntary adventure. Andrew and Tom were delighted that they had safely negotiated the most technically demanding of all the Munros.

On Friday the weather had deteriorated from damp to wet again, so further attempts at mountaineering were abandoned and a final assault was made on Portree to purchase souvenirs (mugs with scenes of Skye summits proved popular). Friday night, however, was a highlight of the week. With the Sligachan Hotel virtually on the doorstep it was the obvious choice of venue for the BSSMC annual dinner. From pre-dinner drinks to fine after dinner Malts, Andrew and Tom may have spoilt the evening for the others by swooning, misty eyed, as they recited the names of famous mountaineers who had used the hotel as a base over the years. The nostalgia outbreak did not affect appetites and the group enjoyed an excellent meal in very pleasant surroundings, at a total cost of £79.95, apparently.

The group failed to find a putting green on Skye for the annual competition - or perhaps it was just too wet for anyone to be bothered, but there was consensus that Graham deserved to win had there been a competition, in recognition of his heroics on the In Pin.

While Andrew, Graham and Roderick returned home next day, Alastair and Tom still had some free time, so Tom elected to visit a couple of hills at Ballachulish, plugging a further gap on the road to "compleation".

Chapter 15

Cairngorms

Andrew and Tom opted for a trip to the Cairngorms in 1992, with Youth Hostels at Loch Morlich and Inverey ideally located for the hills they had in mind. But they had certain memories of the Loch Morlich Hostel which gave them nightmares.

In the early 1970's Andrew, Tom and Donald McNeill had stayed there over a very cold, snowy winter weekend. Much alcohol was consumed and the group's collective behaviour could easily have resulted in a number of bans – from the SYHA, from driving, from having any contact with Boy Scouts and from being allowed anywhere near sardine tins. Their adventures that weekend, in the company of a doctor from Blairgowrie whose attitude to alcohol was less than healthy, are best not recorded.

The week began well for the small BSSMC group of Andrew, Graham and Tom, with a dull, cloudy but dry day for a most enjoyable walk up Bynack More. With no Alastair present to decry the use of mechanical aids, the group took advantage of the chairlift to get to the top of Cairngorm next day for a long walk. They first descended to Loch Avon for a visit to the Shelter Stone, the Holiday Inn of howffs (other hotel chains are available), of which they had read much but had never visited before. Suitably impressed by the number of people who could be accommodated underneath the huge boulder, but glad they would be returning to the comfort of hostel bunk beds that night, they ascended Beinn Mheadhoin, returned to Loch Etchachan for the plod up Derry Cairngorm before returning to the car park over Ben Macdui and Cairngorm – an excellent day.

In need of a break after two fairly strenuous days, the group drove round to Tomintoul to visit Tom's father-in-law, "Winkie" Stewart, who had retired to Balnakyle, a fine traditional villa at the top end of the village. En route they stopped in Aberlour where, after lunch, the annual putting competition took place on a heavily waterlogged putting green, records showing that Andrew won this year.

At Tomintoul they stayed overnight, enjoying Winkie's hospitality and tales from his very varied and interesting careers. Winkie had used a local contact to obtain permission for the group to take a car up the private road in Glen Avon as far as Inchrory, to shorten the climb up Ben Avon from the north. Unfortunately, the day dawned grey and damp but with arrangements having been made they set off regardless, leaving the car at Inchrory as planned and setting off on foot up the higher stretch of the glen. As they left the track to strike up the heather covered shoulder leading to Ben Avon, already in thick cloud, the rain became heavier and only Graham retained any enthusiasm for going on in such weather. Andrew and Tom were not keen to test navigational skills on the plateau of Ben Avon, but they had to force a majority decision on Graham to turn back. Graham seemed to be developing summit syndrome, although his annoyance at being pushed into turning back was understandable considering that it was only a year since he had been pushed into carrying on, in a much more exposed situation and against his better judgement. Returning, wet, to the car they drove round to the Youth Hostel at Inverey for a three night stay. As had been the case at Loch Morlich Hostel, Graham had to hire a sheet sleeping bag as he was not familiar with the custom – generously, this was recorded as a BSSMC expense and therefore the cost was shared.

Cloudy but dry weather on 1st July allowed a long walk up Glen Derry to return over Beinn a Chaorruinn and across the great, spongy alpine moss that is the Moine Bhealaidh, known locally as the "Yalla (yellow?) Moss", where Tom managed to slaughter a family of very young grouse by allowing one of his size 44 Vibram soles to land with considerable force on their nest, an incident he has chosen to erase from his memory by altering certain key facts. The next day was also cold, partly cloudy but dry, ideal conditions for a very long day on Beinn a'Bhuird and Ben Avon, this time using the more conventional approach from Glen Quoich.

There is no record of how the following day was spent but the annual dinner was held in Braemar on the evening of 3rd July. It has long been a point of discussion within the BSSMC as to the venue for the dinner that year. In the BSSMC records there is a receipt for £63.75. The receipt entry of "dinner times 3" implies a Table d'Hote menu and also includes one bottle of the "No 11" and a half bottle of the "No 21." It can be assumed that the bottle was red and was shared by Andrew and Tom while the half bottle, probably of white, was for Graham. The hotel, however, is not named on the bill, which is merely headed with a logo bearing a thistle and the letters MCT. Despite some later detective work by Roderick, the hotel has not been identified beyond reasonable doubt but may have been the Invercauld Arms. Anyone wishing to pursue the issue further may wish to note that the table number was 12 and the waiter was.......squiggle?

The week finished on Saturday 4th July with a walk up the lower stretches of the Lairig Ghru to climb Carn a'Mhaim which, despite being one of the less interesting hills in the Cairngorms, provided a successful conclusion to an enjoyable week.

Chapter 16

Na Tighean Beaga

The venue for the 1993 annual expedition was again chosen to accommodate Andrew and Tom's Munro quest. As the hills they had still to climb were fairly scattered, thought was often given to being able to travel in various directions to take account of weather forecasts for different areas. The area near Spean Bridge had often been identified as a good central base and over the winter of 92/93 a small holiday chalet at Roy Bridge had been booked – "Na Tighean Beaga" (The Little Houses).

The week began on Saturday 26th June with a day which has gone on to become the next BSSMC legend. With Andrew unable to join the group until late that evening, Alastair, Graham and Tom had decided to spend the day on Beinn Achaladair on the way north to Roy Bridge. After what had been a fairly uneventful, successful ascent in good weather, things began to go wrong on the descent and walk back to the car. As was becoming the norm the group had spit into the fast, Alastair and Graham and the not so fast, Tom in this case. Convinced that Tom was behind them, Alastair and Graham stopped at a gate on the path to wait for Tom to catch them up. Meanwhile Tom had cut a corner, joining the path closer to where the car was parked and he was in fact in front of them, already in the car. Eventually, Alastair and Graham decided that something must have happened to Tom and they began to retrace their steps to look for him. Meanwhile, Tom was concluding that something must have happened to the other two and he began to head back along the path to look for them, at least as far as the gate. Had Tom been in the Boy Scouts, rather than the BB, he would have had his Tracker or Backwoodsman Badge, which would have taught him to observe the two sets of bootprints at the gate and deduce what had happened. Meanwhile, with Alastair and Graham having gone back almost as far as the summit without finding Tom they had concluded it was time to return to the farm to call out the Mountain Rescue Team. Thinking along the same lines, Tom had set a 9pm deadline for the other two to turn up and had already alerted a lady at the farm that a rescue call was imminent. At 8.45pm, fifteen minutes before the callout deadline, a time which all three had arrived at independently, the three were re-united at the farm to begin an argument about who did and didn't do what, which has continued annually since. As with all legends there are, of course, differing versions of events.

Finally, late that night, the group of four assembled in the chalet at Na Tighean Beaga. Although the chalet bungalow had been advertised as sleeping four it was a tight squeeze, offering little more space than the residential caravan at Blair Atholl. Tom and Alastair shared one room, Graham had a very small room to himself and Andrew slept on the floor in the living room. With Alastair's sleep being disturbed by Tom's snoring (and whose hasn't?) he spent most nights in his sleeping bag in the small hallway, blocking access from all rooms to the bathroom, as the others discovered when they fell over this great cocoon during nocturnal visits to the toilet, often necessary due to the after effects of evening refreshments.

Exhausted by their efforts to locate Tom the previous day, Alastair and Graham opted for a rest day on Sunday before the whole group climbed two fairly forgettable hills to the north of Loch Moy on Monday. In clean boots and socks, Andrew began the day with an early plunge into filthy, wet peat, providing the others with their highlight of the day - a performance he has repeated often since.

Tuesday was wet. Nevertheless Andrew, Graham and Tom decided to drive out to Glen Dessary, hoping the weather would clear on the way out. Alastair elected to have a day off and Graham probably wished he had too, as he did not enjoy being the back seat passenger on the long and winding road. At the road end there was one of these situations where each person took it in turn to assess whether the rain was easing, leading to endless discussion about whether to leave the shelter of the car or not. As they took turns at winding down their steamed up windows to check the status of the rain, the decision to leave the car was deferred for as long as possible and then some more. Eventually they set off for an enjoyable, if damp day on three hills to the west, culminating in Sgurr na Ciche. Disappointingly, there was no view from this fine peak.

Alastair replaced Graham next day as back seat passenger. Graham was nursing some fairly serious blisters and had already been up Gulvain, so he had opted out of the drive to Glenfinnan. The other three enjoyed a sunny but cold, windy day with excellent views from Gulvain.

What happened on the Thursday and Friday is not recorded, presumably because the weather had deteriorated or the injury list had grown, but there would, undoubtedly, have been the obligatory pilgrimage to the Parallel Roads of Glen Roy. There is also evidence of at least one festering day in Fort William in the annual accounts, with coffees, lunches and even afternoon teas being recorded. This had been the year in which the BSSMC had made a collective purchase of a board game called "Munro Mania," a sort of Trivial Pursuit around the Munros. It was played at least once but doesn't seem to have been particularly popular.

At the end of the week the group moved base to the nearby Youth Hostel at Loch Lochy for three further days. The outlying Mamore summit, Binnean Beag was climbed via a very boggy path at the head of Glen Nevis. Then Graham was persuaded, by offering him the front passenger seat in the car, to undertake a return journey along the Loch Arkaig switchback to Glen Dessary for a cold and windy ascent of Sgurr Mor.

Finally, the group took a car to the remote hotel above the north shore of Loch Leven where they experienced a déjà vu of the scene in 1988. The "hotel" was full of similar skeletal geriatrics, still sitting asleep or wandering aimlessly along the corridors. With some hesitation, coffee was purchased, although no one had the inclination to linger long, and a parking fee of £1.50 (a much more formal arrangement than in 1988) was paid before the group set off for a pleasant day on two summits in the Mamores which no one was terribly sure they had been up before. There was a certain determination that there would be no cheating when the final tick came to be put on the Munro list.

Chapter 17

Sunshine on Skye

Since their experience of Skye in the rain in 1991 no one in the BSSMC had expressed any great enthusiasm for a return trip. Andrew and Tom were, however, well aware that if they were to climb all the Munros a return trip was inevitable sooner or later. May or June remained the best options, but June had been pretty disastrous before so a bold decision was made to try May. Unfortunately that suited only Andrew, Graham and Tom so once again it was a small, select group which set off on 6th May 1994 on the ferry from Kyle of Lochalsh – a much more interesting approach than today's bridge. They pretended to be ignoring the clear, sunny weather as they crossed over to Skye and drove north to a privately run hostel at Staffin. Was this going to be the one good day?

The hostel, run by an immigrant Yorkshireman and his wife, was a series of linked Nissen huts which although quite unsightly from outside offered comfortable accommodation, with ample cooking, eating and lounge facilities and good toilets and showers. Being some way away from the Cuillins it was not too busy either.

It seemed unlikely that there would be any "easy" days on Skye, but there was general agreement that Bruach na Frith offered the most straightforward start to the week, being little more than a walk. Sunday 7th May dawned cold but bright – ideal conditions. Starting from the road just above Sligachan and following a good path, the summit of Bruach na Frith was gained with ease, perhaps instilling a false sense of security in the minds of the two older BSSMC members. From the summit, the group was able to see the Main Ridge in detail for the first time – in 1991 they hadn't been able to see it at all. It looked magnificent from this particularly good viewpoint, with fair amounts of snow lying in the gullies and corries. Fortunately they had brought ice axes and it would not be long until they were to be of use. The technical difficulties of the Bhasteir Tooth ruled out any direct route to Am Basteir, the second planned summit of the day, but tracks through the snow in the corries to the north of Am Basteir suggested a possible route. The snow was in ideal condition, allowing easy progress, as the group contoured round steep slopes into Coire a' Bhasteir and up steep snow to Bealach a' Bhasteir. From here the route was via the East Ridge, graded RII in the guidebook (or Moderate rock climbing in old money) which Andrew and Tom reckoned to be about the limit of their ability now. The ridge proved to be reasonably straightforward, apart from a short descent which involved a bit of a stretch. Graham jumped part way down, Tom dreeped, using as much friction as possible to keep him attached to the rock, Andrew managed to fall off, landing on his backside. The summit was reached without further incident and the return along the ridge was easier. A very successful first day, which left a long lasting impression on Andrew's left hip, finished with a pleasant descent through snow and an easy walk back to Sligachan for a well earned pint.

Much to everyone's surprise and delight the dry sunny weather continued next day, so the group made an early start and drove to Glenbrittle for the long walk into Coir' a' Ghrunnda. A fairly easy climb and walk out to Sgurr nan Eag, the most southerly Munro on the Main Ridge, was followed by a return to Bealach a'Gharbh-choire, where the tricky traverse of Caisteal a'Garbh Choire was avoided by contouring to the west, with magnificent views back to Loch Skavaig. From here there was a steep scramble up well scratched rock on the south face of Sgurr Dubh Mor, whose summit table was so small that Andrew, Graham and Tom had to take turns to stand on it, each posing for photographs against a magnificent mountain backdrop and BLUE SKY!!

The weather gods continued to look kindly on all those fortunate enough to be on Skye that second week of May. So as a further sunny day dawned on Tuesday, the group returned to Glenbrittle for an ascent of Sgurr Alasdair. Having scoured the guidebooks for a viable alternative to the Great Stone Shoot (or should that be Chute?) and failing, they walked into Coire Lagan, hoping from what they had seen so far that there might be some snow to aid progress. Despite the cold wind, the walk into Coire Lagan was so much more enjoyable than the wet trauchle it had been in 1991. And this time they kept to the path above the huge slabs on which they had floundered about in the rain before, locating the lochan successfully and considering with amazement where they might have been in 1991. Pausing to watch climbers on the huge cliffs above and on the Cioch, Andrew and Tom's admiration for Jim Cathcart grew enormously, Jim having climbed the Cioch some years before. Jim claims he had had to be dragged up by Bob Campbell, the most competent climber among his friends but, even so, the sheer exposure of the place would scare the wits out of a dead sheep and involve most folk in several changes of underwear.

Having heard horrible tales of the 1000 feet slog up the tumbling treadmill of loose scree which fills the Great Stone Chute (or should that be Shoot?) and which cannot be avoided easily, they were astonished to turn in to the bottom of the gully to find it full, from top to bottom, of firm snow which allowed an enjoyable ascent with some step cutting near the top, from where they emerged into sunshine, clear blue skies and a cold wind. Following a preliminary scouting mission by Graham, all three made their way up the east ridge, an exposed but not too difficult scramble, to reach the summit of Sgurr Alasdair and more magnificent views. The snow in the Stone Chute (or should that be......) allowed a running/glissading descent, in Tom's case at least partially involuntarily, almost all the way down to the corrie, where a long sunbathing rest seemed in order. The water looked inviting and Graham revealed that he had swimming trunks with him. Apparently his mother had always, since he started going away on the hills as a teenager, insisted that he pack swimming trunks "just in case". Here was the perfect chance to try them out. With considerable encouragement from the others, Graham disappeared to the gents' changing rooms to re-appear wearing the most ridiculously brief "Speedos". The water was, of course, too cold to go in, but Graham posed for photos, perched on rocks above the lochan. Heaven knows what climbers looking down from the Cioch must have made of this strange scene. Graham's trunks have not been in evidence on any subsequent BSSMC expedition.

The spell of settled weather and consequent busy schedule on the hills meant that there had been no time for a rest day. Any spare time had been spent on mundane matters such as buying food, eating and sleeping. Even visits to the nearby pub tended to be of brief duration.

Any visitor to Skye could hardly fail to notice that the island is being run by English settlers, with varying degrees of sympathy to local tradition and with varying degrees of success. But one small incident, witnessed by the BSSMC group, suggested that a new generation of Skye man may be developing. It was about 8pm with the long May day leaving darkness still a long way off. The hostel owner was shouting to his young son, who was some way down the road, to come in to do his homework or some other tedious domestic chore. In response to his dad's instruction, which was delivered in his broad Yorkshire brogue, the young lad, in a fairly authentic West Highland lilt replied, "But Dad, I have to go to shinty practice," as he wielded his caman.

Unbelievably, the settled weather was still holding, so there was no excuse for not tackling the remaining tops. The road to Glenbrittle was becoming familiar by now, but the beautiful morning light which illuminated the tops of the Main Ridge ensured continuing enthusiasm on the journey and frequent stops for photographs each day. Sgurr na Banachdich was the next hill to be tackled. Across the road from Glenbrittle Youth Hostel a good path led uphill beside the Coire a Ghreadaidh burn, followed by a more sketchy path into Coir' an Eich. From here it was a fairly straightforward walk to the summit with a return by the same route.

The now expected cold, dry, sunny weather continued for yet another trip to Glenbrittle and up the same path as the previous day, but this time continuing high into Coire a Ghreadaidh for the approach to An Dorus (The Door). This route had been causing Andrew and Tom some concern as the guidebooks described a short but steep step out of the narrow gap and on to the ridge leading up to the summit of Sgurr a' Mhadaidh and an even more difficult pitch out of the notch on the way south to Sgurr a'Ghreadaidh. On their arrival at The Door, an obvious lunch venue, the group couldn't really identify either of these difficulties. Luckily, snow was lying to a sufficient depth to fill in the lower parts of the difficult pitches which had become no more than long steps on to good rock. So, short scrambles led to each top in turn and the day was again one of good scrambling and superb views.

At this point, the reader may pause to wonder why, after sixteen chapters containing very little by way of detailed routes followed, descriptions of routes taken should appear now. Well, it is intended to show anyone put off the hills of Skye by stories of technical difficulties that if Andrew and Tom managed these routes, albeit with a "minder", anyone should be able to cope. The risk in such detail is, of course, that one might think it had been lifted from a guidebook and that the BSSMC had never..........

By all accounts, Sgurr Mhich Coinnich would be a serious challenge, so it was no coincidence that it had been left until last. Fortunately the excellent weather continued to provide ideal conditions for a fifth consecutive trip to Glenbrittle. Why had they not just stayed in Glenbrittle in the first place? The thinking seems to have been that if they had encountered typically wet Skye weather there was nothing they could do there and being forced out of the hostel each day in the rain would be a drag. Whereas staying nearer Portree at least offered a few cafes and pubs to while away wet hours. Perhaps such thinking should always be applied if the result is a week of magnificent weather.

The chosen route to Sgurr Mhich Coinnich was via Coire Lagan and the steep scree slopes of An Stac to Bealach Lagan. Lots of group photographs were taken at this particularly scenic spot before Graham set off in front along the long, narrow ridge leading to the summit. The climb was not particularly difficult but the rock seemed always to slope dangerously towards huge voids of Poucherian precipitousness to the east. Maintaining as much contact with the rock as possible, the group reached the very exposed summit, returning cautiously by the same route to the bealach. Having successfully completed all the summits on the Main Ridge, Andrew, Graham and Tom took it in turns to try to kill each other by dislodging large stones as they ran or stumbled down the long scree slope, for a final linger by the loch in Coire Lagan.

By the end of such a busy week, Andrew and Tom's fingers and knees were skint and raw from frequent multi-point contact with the coarse and abrasive Skye gabbro. Both were happy to acknowledge that without Graham as their explorer, guide, mentor and nanny, it is unlikely that they would have been able to reach several of the summits. And they wondered what they had done to deserve such perfect weather conditions.

The venue for the annual dinner had to be the Sligachan Hotel on the Friday evening. At a total cost of £92.25 it must be assumed that the bill included a drink or two. The dinner was a fitting end to a memorable week – but it wasn't quite over.

With the Saturday being sunny and even warmer than the rest of the week, the group decided to return home via the ferry from Kylerhea to Glenelg for a relentless slog up Ben Sgritheall. It was hot, hazy and very sweaty. Graham was rewarded for his efforts earlier in the week by becoming the unwitting host to the entire tick population of the mountain who thought he might take them up the hill too. On the descent, a grooming session near the car relieved Graham of his unwelcome visitors.

The weather conditions for the week could not have been kinder and the large quantities of late snow had made conditions ideal for ascents via gullies. Maybe Skye isn't such a horrible place after all.

Top of The Great Stone Chute, Skye

Chapter 18

When Alastair Met Marion And Coronach Played The Ceilidh Place

Andrew and Tom had, by now, climbed around 250 Munros and could see "compleation" on the not too distant horizon so they had decided this was the year to plug some more gaps in their respective repertoires. Once again Youth Hostels provided the best options and, with Alastair and Graham, they set off for Ullapool on Saturday 9th June 1995. They travelled north via Inverness, where they did some shopping then, deciding the good weather was too good to waste in transit, they stopped at the Aultguish Inn for lunch, phoned ahead to Ullapool Youth Hostel to warn of a late arrival, then set off for a very pleasant, late afternoon ascent of Am Faochagach via Loch Vaich. This was a much more enjoyable route than the one taken in the aborted attempt in 1989 through heather and bog above Loch Glascarnoch. Alastair attempted to bring his unique approach to the day by heading off in a direct line for the summit. Unfortunately it was not the summit of Am Faochagach but, as it was a summit in Alastair's line of sight, it was good enough for him. Fortunately the others were able to rein him in before he had gone too far in the wrong ("different," according to Alastair) direction.

After a late arrival at Ullapool Youth Hostel, Sunday saw the group split. Alastair and Tom drove to the Fannichs to enable Tom to climb an outlying summit, Sgurr nan Each, which he had missed on previous visits. Meanwhile Andrew and Graham walked up Glean na Sguaib (it was no longer possible to take a car up into the forest – presumably increases in numbers using this shortcut to the hill had resulted in the access gate being locked). Graham climbed Beinn Dearg while Andrew waited for him at the bealach, then both walked out to Cona Mheall, which Andrew had missed way back in 1979. The two groups met back at the hostel for dinner.

The real entertainment of the day, however, was to be reserved for the evening. Tom had been in touch with Cathy Niven and had learned that the band in which she and her husband, Roger, played was due to perform in the Ceilidh Place that evening. The band, Coronach, played a range of medieval and renaissance music on a range of medieval and renaissance instruments. Perhaps not everyone's cup of tea, but Tom assured the others that they were very accomplished musicians so the others agreed they would attend. Needless to say a few pints of liquid were consumed at the bar in the Ceilidh Place before the group crossed the road to the concert venue. Apart from the BSSMC members there was an English family of four plus two or three other people at most making up the audience. The concert was very good and there was even an interval to allow time for more liquid refreshment. This, however, was to be Tom's downfall. For much of the second half his legs were crossed in a vice like grip as a polite alternative to a disruptive departure to visit the gents'. The concert ended to rapturous applause from the audience. As the applause died, Tom rose to pursue relief from his growing discomfort, but the band responded to the applause by offering to perform an encore. Tom felt obliged to resume his cross legged position and by now holding his breath too he was only just able to avoid an embarrassing incident. At last, on the final note of the encore, Tom was able to race to the gents' with a sigh of relief. Few have ever witnessed Tom move so fast. The BSSMC and Coronach joined forces for a late night drink in the residents' lounge at the Ceilidh Place, where the band was staying overnight.

Amazingly, the group was fit enough next morning to tackle a very long day on Seana Braigh. The chosen route was from Inverlael via Glen na Sguaib and a path, which varied in quality, across mile after mile of open ground into Coire an Lochain Sgeirich and on to the bealach above Gleann a' Chadha Dheirg before a final walk up a broad, curving ridge to the summit. The prospect of having to return by the same route was daunting, but the weather was kind, being mainly dry and cool. The weather didn't make the return any shorter, though. Seana Braigh is one of the most remote Munros so it was satisfying to have climbed it before old age took any more of a toll.

Back at the hostel Andrew had recognised a member of another mountaineering group which had been sharing the hostel – Marion MacFarlane, whom he knew from his place of work, Argyle House in Edinburgh. She had been pursuing her Munro bagging career for only a few years but she and her companions were rapidly approaching "compleation". Andrew introduced her to the others and, although the two groups bumped into each other in the pub over the week, there was no real interaction. Some years later, Andrew and Marion were travelling together by train from Edinburgh to Glasgow to attend a meeting. Sharing a common interest, it was natural that the conversation turned quickly to mountains and travel and it was not long until Alastair's name cropped up as the most widely travelled member of the BSSMC and perhaps a good source of advice. To cut a long story short, Andrew unwittingly acted as a conduit which led to a long standing relationship between Alastair and Marion - well, at least every second month when Alastair returned from his work, often from places with unpronounceable names. On December 21st 2010, they married.

Anyway, back to Ullapool. Tuesday 12th June was a warm, sunny day, so the group drove to Dundonnell for a full and entertaining traverse of An Teallach – a great day. Alastair drew a few passing glances as he had discarded his boots, which had been causing him some discomfort, in favour of a pair of brown walking shoes, albeit with a decent sole, which he claimed were completely fit for purpose. The whole ridge was completed in excellent weather, with Graham even taking time to write a few postcards at 3000 feet.

Due to the fact that Graham was having to leave the group next day to travel to a conference in Greece – shame! – the BSSMC annual dinner was held in the Ceilidh Place that evening. Things started well enough, until Alastair, perhaps distracted by a rather attractive young waitress, spilled a full pint of beer, over Tom mostly. Tom was forced into an embarrassing dash into the gents toilet (his second dash of the week to a toilet), passing other drinkers who glanced suspiciously at the large wet patch on the front of his trousers. Fortunately, his trousers were the legendary Rohan Bags which, after ten minutes of contortions beneath the warm air drier (later copied by Rowan Atkinson in one of his Mr. Bean escapades), had dried out sufficiently for Tom to take his place with the others in the dining room. The meal was excellent, but fellow diners had their pleasant evening shattered by some loud, alcohol-fuelled argument at the BSSMC table, by now a BSSMC tradition.

Next day the group travelled to Fort William, where Graham was transferred to public transport to begin his journey to Greece. His early departure necessitated early closure of the BSSMC annual account and a Part II account was opened for the remainder of the week. Those with an interest in how such meticulous record keeping was conducted will be intrigued to know that the main account was kept on a bright yellow page from Tom's filofax, while the Part II account was kept on a light green page.

Andrew, Alastair and Tom then checked into Loch Lochy Youth Hostel from where, next day, they drove out to Glenfinnan for an excellent day on Sgurr Thuilm and Sgurr Nan Coireachan in sunny, but quite cold weather. From there it was on to Glencoe Hostel, busy as always, for two days on hills in Glen Etive and finally another trip up the hill by chairlift to allow Andrew, this time, to tick off the summit of Creise, which had been elevated to Munro status since days in the 1970s when the hills of the Blackmount had been visited regularly. Maybe Creise had been visited, but nothing was being left to chance now.

On the Friday night there was a second, unofficial annual dinner, in the Clachaig Inn. By the end of this week, Andrew and Tom were very close to having been up the same hills in total, but it was clear that visiting the few remaining summits would take careful planning, as there were still a few very remote tops to be climbed.

Chapter 19

Boats and Bikes

A new member joined the BSSMC for its 1996 Annual Expedition. Paul Forrest, younger son of a work colleague and friend of Andrew's, was in his late teens and keen to get out into the hills but his group of friends, whose main interests were skiing and snowboarding, were less enthusiastic about hillwalking so Paul was prepared to throw his lot in with this elderly group. Andrew and Paul travelled to Fort William where Paul was introduced to Graham and Tom over a traditional BSSMC opening lunch at the West End Hotel. Although there are no records to confirm it, Graham probably ate scampi and chips. Bookmakers throughout Scotland had long since stopped accepting bets on that one.

From Fort William the group drove to Cannich Youth Hostel as a base for their first few days. Unfortunately, back in 1982, Andrew and Tom had left Beinn Fhionnlaidh, an outlier of Carn Eige, unclimbed during a very wet day in the area. The plan for the first day was for a long day on the Glen Affric hills to include the aforementioned outlier. The day started well enough during the long walk in and for the ascent of Carn Eige and out to Bheinn Fhionnlaidh. On the return trip over Carn Eige it began to rain, but there was agreement that Mam Sodhail should be visited regardless. As the group began the descent from the bealach between the two major tops it was becoming very wet and the long walk down the vague path by the swollen burn seemed never ending. By the time they reached the track near Affric Lodge everyone was soaked and Paul's enthusiasm for the hills was taking a serious knock, with still a long way to go to the car.

Later that evening, having confirmed that the weather forecast for the next day was good, a phone call was made to a Dutch gentleman who owned a small boat on Loch Mullardoch and seemed to have cornered the market in ferrying Munro baggers to the top of the loch to allow an easier day on the remote tops to the north of the loch. He confirmed he was available next day to act as BSSMC ferryman. Goodness knows what Alastair would have made of such assistance. Tom was not particularly thrilled by the prospect of a boat trip either – he is not happy in this mode of transport (rather ironic since in his later years he has served as resident geologist on ships sailing to the Arctic and Antarctic through some of the roughest waters in the world).

So, at 9am next morning the BSSMC assembled on a small beach next to the dam on Loch Mullardoch, met the Dutchman and jumped aboard his small launch for the 30 minute trip up the loch. Strong headwinds whipped up waves big enough to remind Tom that he was not a sailor, but Paul seemed much happier, getting wet this time only from the spray breaking over the tiny cabin in which they were huddled together. The remoteness of the location hit home as the boatman put them ashore in a small bay on the north shore of the loch, below a long spur leading up to An Socath, before turning his boat around and sailing back down the loch. As the sound of the engine faded the only sign of civilisation was a small, but very smart, wooden chalet built near the burn and protected by a deer fence. Quickly leaving this remote hideaway behind they walked up the long spur leading to An Socath, one of the most remote of all the Munros, with views of high tops in all directions. A long ridge walk over the three further summits followed in cold but dry conditions, with just enough low cloud to challenge route finding skills on what was quite a complicated ridge in places. It was a most enjoyable day, ending back at the dam, where it was clear that Paul's faith in mountaineering as an enjoyable pastime had been, at least in part, restored.

Having completed all the summits in the Glen Affric area, Andrew and Tom were keen to press on to Braemar, where a couple of remote summits to the south of Glen Geldie had eluded them to date and which remained a major hurdle en route to "compleation". So Tuesday was spent driving to Braemar Youth Hostel, making a slight detour to visit Paul's parents who were holidaying in a friend's chalet near Contin. Perhaps concerned that the BSSMC had not been feeding her son adequately, Paul's mum, Sana, set to preparing bacon rolls for the group, which were much appreciated since it had been at least an hour since they had eaten breakfast!

Bacon has been the subject of much discussion over the years, particularly how well it has to be cooked to satisfy individual demands. Everyone in the BSSMC insists that as much fat as possible must be cut off before the bacon is grilled – never fried. Tom insists that the bacon must be cut thick; he will not entertain the wafer thin, pre-packed, watery stuff available in most supermarkets. He also insists his bacon must not be overcooked while, at the other extreme, Graham's must be incinerated. In between, in order of time under the grill, come Paul, Alastair and Andrew. Sana's bacon seemed to meet with general approval.

Fortified for the journey to Braemar – to which there is no obvious direct route from Contin, the group called in at Dingwall for more provisions, lunched in Tomintoul and arrived at Braemar Youth Hostel in time for dinner. They fed well that day.

Tom had been up Lochnagar before but Andrew hadn't so, with Tom's knee giving him trouble, he undertook a short amble in the area while the three others set off for a long day on the five Munros which make up Lochnagar and the White Mounth. Fortunately, visibility was good for most of the day allowing good progress. The building clouds in the afternoon provided a magnificent skyscape but also brought the threat of rain. On the long walk down Loch Muick the clouds chose to empty their entire contents leading to three very wet but content walkers.

On the way to Loch Muick Tom was nearly forced off the road by two Range Rovers, the first driven by a gentleman who bore more than a passing resemblance to Prince Charles, the second being driven by a Camilla Parker-Bowles lookalike. This was long before any relationship between the two had become public knowledge.

Attention then turned to the hills in Glen Geldie. These are a long way from anywhere and unless tents were to be used the other feasible option permitting a day trip was the use of mountain bikes. This had been discussed in previous years but had been dismissed by Andrew, as he had never learned to ride a bicycle (as a child he had failed to graduate from his much loved tri-cycle). However he had purchased a bike the previous year and could just about stay upright. Tom's enthusiasm for two wheels was not great either, having not long recovered from a broken wrist following a somersault over the handlebars of his bike on his way home from work. Graham, on the other hand, was enthusiastic, although he was much more at home on a road bike. Paul, however, was relishing the idea, as he was a mountain bike enthusiast. There was an outdoor shop in Braemar from which mountain bikes could be hired, so the group of four was at its front door as it opened on the morning of 5th July to rent the wheels. The bikes were bundled into the backs of cars for the short journey to Linn O' Dee, where the BSSMC Cycling Club made a very shoogly start up the landrover track towards White Bridge.

For most of the way the bike was more of a hindrance than a help to Andrew, who spent a lot of time falling off, remounting, dismounting, pushing and cursing. Tom fared slightly better, while Graham and Paul were enjoying the ride. Finally the bikes were abandoned at the ford where the path crossed to the "Geldie Hotel", the misleading nickname given to a bothy there. From here it was no more than a long plod round the two remote summits. Andrew fared marginally better on his bike on the return trip, mainly downhill. It had been a long day and, having first returned the bikes, the group took little persuading to eat in the bar of the Fife Arms Hotel, which was just about to stop serving meals as they arrived.

Out on its own to the east, Mount Keen is unique in being the only Munro to bear the title "Mount". There were two possible approaches. The first involved a long walk up Glen Tanar, probably the more scenic route, while the alternative from Glen Mark was much shorter but would involve a long drive from Braemar to Ballater, over the Cairn O' Mounth to Fettercairn, Edzell and the long drag up the narrow road in Glen Esk. Guess which option the BSSMC chose? The long drive and easy walk, of course. It was going to be a long day.

Being the last day of the trip, some plans had to be made for the annual dinner. There is a small hotel by the roadside at Inver, half way between

Braemar and Ballater which looked interesting and would be on the road home later, so it was agreed it might be worth considering.

Andrew was nominated to go in to the hotel to appraise the suitability of the menu for the BSSMC dinner. With no sign of a menu on display, he made his way through to what seemed to be a lounge bar. Still no menu and no one around to ask. Some noisy shuffling and a cough or two brought a small, elderly lady from a door at the side of the bar to enquire if she could help. Her Buchan accent identified her as a "real" local and not simply an imported student working for the season, so that was a good start.

"Do you have a dinner menu for this evening which I could look at please?" asked Andrew.

"Thirs nae menu oot yet son, but its aye the same," was the response.

"Well, can you give me some idea of what might be on, so that my friends and I can decide if we'd like to eat here this evening?"

"Weel, there'll be soup. There's aye soup. An' there'll be melin, aye. Oh aye, an' prawn coacktail. Then we'll hae beef, maybe steak pie, an' chicken, there's aye chicken. An' likely fish. Oh aye, fish. Then thirs desserts."

Somewhat surprised at the extent and variety of the menu and the mouth-watering descriptions, Andrew asked, "Is that the menu for the bar, or is it for the dining room?"

"Oh, ye can hae it in the bar, or the dining room. In fact, ye can hae it ootside fur aw ah care. It's aw the same."

Andrew thanked the lady for her help, muttered something about having to consult his friends and made a hasty retreat to the car. The BSSMC elected not eat there.

The long journey over the Cairn o' Mounth road to Fettercairn and Edzell left everyone in need of a short break at Edzell where some supplies were purchased. The break, however, did little to dispel the growing discomfort of car sickness being experienced by the back seat passengers, Graham and Paul, who were absolutely delighted to arrive finally at the small car park at Invermark, starting point for the day's walk.

The remainder of the day was very enjoyable, beginning with the pleasant walk up Glen Mark to the Queen's Well, an ornate granite canopy covering a well, commemorating a spot where Queen Victoria rested on her crossing of the Mounth track with Prince Albert in 1861. Apart from the steep zig-zag part of the path known as "The Ladder," the route was an easy walk, with fine views all around. On the return journey sightings of red squirrels and an adult adder on the path rounded off the day nicely. The return journey to Braemar was more leisurely for the sake of the back seat passengers.

The earlier rejection of the non existent menu at the Inver Hotel led to Tom suggesting the Invercauld Arms in Braemar as a venue. It had looked a bit grey from the outside and hinted that it might be over priced, but the others accepted Tom's advice that having eaten there before, he thought it would be fine. Andrew and Graham appear to have had no recollection that they may have eaten there before, so Tom cannot be held totally responsible for the choice of venue. The meal began badly with menus being proffered by waitresses who clearly did not speak English – a bit like the lady earlier, but this time the accent was Eastern European. The food which arrived didn't necessarily coincide with the food which was ordered and not timeously either. The head waiter tried to make feeble excuses that he was having to train new staff, but he was rarely around when they needed help. Having decided not to leave a tip because of the dreadfully poor service, the group retired to a very tartan residents' lounge for after dinner drinks and the annual BSSMC argument. Paul was shocked by the lack of regard for the two or three other people in the lounge who couldn't have failed to hear every word. He soon came to understand that the annual argument is an integral part of each year's get together.

Paul's introduction to the BSSMC way of life concluded next day just outside Perth, where the annual accounts were finalised over coffee in the, now closed, Caithness Glass visitor centre.

The Cliffs of Lochnagar

Chapter 20

The Final Countdown

Much discussion took place over the winter of 1996/97 regarding whether it would be possible for Andrew and Tom to finish their Munro quest during the summer of '97 or whether it would need a further year. It was concluded that if it was possible to climb five Munros near Achnashellach and one in Kintail early in June, it would then be possible to proceed to Mull to climb Ben More, possibly in July.

The Achnashellach area was difficult from an accommodation point of view. Given Alastair and Tom's previous experience at a nearby private hostel, the group would not be staying there – even assuming it were still open, so the chosen starting point was the Youth Hostel at Ratagan. Alastair, Andrew, Graham, Paul and Tom assembled on Wednesday 11th June, a midweek departure having been chosen to accommodate the increasingly busy diaries of the participants, and drove to Kintail. On arrival, Alastair donated a bottle of Macallan to the group, as payment of his debt for non-attendance the previous year. He insisted that it be placed on record that his debt had been paid in full, with "honour and ceremony."

Plans were made for the next day. The ascent of Sgurr Choinnich and Sgurr a' Chaorachain involved a fairly long walk in from the railway level crossing at Craig. This was a walk that would have to be repeated later in the week for the ascent of Maoile Lunndaidh and thoughts were turning to ways of making it less arduous. It was a cold day, with low cloud and some light drizzle, but it gave a successful start to the week.

The weather was poor next day, but that allowed the group to drive to Torridon Youth Hostel. Given that they were planning to go back to Craig next day it seems strange they didn't just stay on at Ratagan, or head straight to Torridon from the outset. But such are the unpredictable ways of the BSSMC!

Saturday had been earmarked for the ascent of Maoile Lunndaidh. Passing through Lochcarron on the Friday, a bicycle hire business had been spotted and bikes had been booked for the Saturday to ease the walk in. Bikes were duly collected and transported by car to the starting point at Craig. Alastair declined the opportunity to use a bike and as he strode ahead of Andrew and Tom, who were struggling to pedal uphill, they couldn't help think that Alastair might have made a wise decision. Then he began to catch Paul, who had set off at a cracking pace, but whose bike had begun to fall apart. He had dismounted and was trying to repair a broken pedal as Alastair passed. Graham was the only cyclist who reached the bothy, where the bikes were to be left, ahead of Alastair. The others arrived later, Andrew pushing rather than struggling to pedal, Paul limply depressing his only good pedal ("He was having trouble with his crank" according to Graham) and Tom wobbling as he made slow, but determined progress. The bikes were abandoned behind the bothy and more conventional methods were adopted for the ascent of Maoile Lunndaidh. The long descent saw Graham race off on his bike to be first back at the car – only to be eaten alive by midges as he waited for the others. Alastair kept pace with the others, who occasionally gained a few yards' advantage where free wheeling was possible. While the day on the hill was declared a success, the use of rented bikes seemed to have caused more bother than they were worth, at a cost of £47.50!!

Most of the day on Sunday was spent relaxing from the previous day's efforts and preparing for the major expedition of the week, a visit to the remote summits of Bidean a' Choire Sheasgaich (often referred to as "Cheesecake" by Munro baggers). The main meal of the day was taken at lunchtime in Lochcarron before rucksacks were packed for the walk in to Bernais bothy. Arriving late in the evening they found the bothy occupied by two fishermen using it as a base to fish some remote hill lochs, but still leaving plenty room on the floor. It was a particularly uncomfortable night for Graham, who had been unaware that he would need a sleeping bag this week. He slept (sort of) inside his rucksack, inside a bivvy bag. Graham's recollection - "It was Baltic!!!" To add insult to injury, he was lying next to Tom, who had clearly decided to make one of his famous attempts at two world snoring records – for volume and duration. In his defence, Tom hadn't been feeling well and it was discovered later that he had been displaying early symptoms of Lyme disease which he had contracted on a trip to USA a month or so earlier.

Fortunately Monday dawned sunny and pleasantly warm. After breakfast cooked on Primus stoves, which the BSSMC members, other than Alastair, had not used for many years, they set off for an excellent day on the two remote summits of the "Cheesecake" and its neighbour, Lurg Mhor. Collecting the rest of their gear from the bothy on the way past, they made the long walk out in the late afternoon. This was one of these occasions when Alastair elected to baffle the others with his choice of footwear - one boot and one shoe (he had a sore foot).

The group drove back to Ratagan Youth Hostel that evening and on to the annual dinner in the Kintail Lodge Hotel. Everyone was pretty tired after the discomfort of the bothy and the long day, but the meal was most enjoyable. Some group members even tried their hand at darts after the meal. Their skill levels can be judged by how the game ended, nearest the board wins! Tom experienced another uncomfortable night of extreme sweating as his Lyme disease developed.

Tom hadn't been up Bheinn Fhada (Ben Attow), so Tuesday 17th saw the group set off from Morvich for a traverse of the long ridge in warm but windy conditions. At several points they met a very well equipped lone walker who, despite careful scrutiny of his map had been about to head off in the wrong direction on at least two occasions. Fortunately he had had the good sense to consult the collective mountain of knowledge that is the BSSMC and was pointed in the right direction.

Now the scene was set for Tom and Andrew to "compleat" the Munros with an ascent of Ben More on Mull – the planning had already begun.

The Saddle from Glen Shiel

Chapter 21

"Compleation" on Mull

Plans were made for a long weekend on Mull to enable Andrew and Tom to climb Ben More, their final Munro, together. Some reconnaissance work had been done earlier in the year when Andrew and Audrey had visited Mull for a weekend. Invitations would be sent to those who had had significant involvement with Andrew and Tom on the hills over the years, to join the "final" ascent and to celebrate with a meal afterwards. Tobermory was judged to be the best base and to offer the best options for a, hopefully, celebratory meal. So, the following invitation was sent out:-

B.S.S.M.C.

~~~~000~~~~

The Chairman and Board of Management of B.S.S.M.C. request the Pleasure of your Company at a levee to be held on Friday 11th July 1997 on the Peak of Ben More on the Island of Mull to celebrate the Completion by Messrs A. Vickery and T. Sharpe of a Sustained Campaign over a Quarter of a Century of the Ascent of those Summits tabulated by Sir Hugh T. Munro Bt.

Two routes are available: the Classic Ascent *via* A'Chioch for Alpinistes and a Pedestrian route for Camp followers, Servants, Flunkeys, Lackeys and Skivvies.

Upon successful completion of the Expedition, the Party will retire to a Licensed Hostelry where Intoxicating Beverages will be imbibed followed by Celebratory Epulation.

In the event of Inclement Weather, the Party will make the Ascent on the day following.

Upon receipt of Expression of your Intention to attend, further details of the Arrangements will be forwarded.

A number of people accepted the invitation and made significant efforts to get to Mull to join in the celebrations. Jim and Susan Cathcart built the weekend into a caravanning trip to Mull, basing themselves at the site in Craignure. Donald and Linda Cameron drove north from Wigtown to spend the weekend in a B&B in Tobermory. Roderick brought his wife Karen and their three teenagers, Joy, Ronnie and Neil for a holiday in Scotland, also spending the weekend in a B&B in Tobermory. Graham and his partner Tina stayed at another B&B in Tobermory. Paul travelled over on the ferry with Audrey and Andrew, leaving his car in Oban where he forgot to pay for parking in his rush to catch the boat. He had brought a tent with him and camped in a basic site on a small farm just outside Tobermory. Andrew, Audrey, Tom and Jennifer had decided to stay in the comparative luxury of The Tobermory Hotel, a very comfortable, small hotel in a central location on Tobermory's waterfront. Apologies were received from Alastair, Cathy and Roger Niven, Bill and Jean Brown and Mike McGinnes.

As they met up for a hearty cooked breakfast on the morning of 11th July 1997, Andrew and Tom marvelled that the day had arrived when they would, barring accidents or severe weather problems, become "Munroists". Over breakfast final details of the plan for the day were discussed. The weather was fairly benign – dry, fairly warm, hazy, little sunshine but little cloud either, at least over Tobermory. Everyone taking part in the day's climb had agreed to meet at a parking place near the croft of Dhiseig on the south shore of Loch na Keal for a 10 am start. Group photographs taken in hazy sunshine by the side of the loch delayed the start until about 10.30. The non-climbers, Audrey and Linda Cameron, drove off for a tour of the coffee and craft shops of Mull, Roderick and Karen took the walkers path leading directly to the summit of Ben More via its north west ridge, laden with supplies for the summit celebrations, while the main group of 12 set off up a vague path into Gleann na Beinne Fada and the on to the north ridge of A'Chioch.

A stubborn cloud sat on the summit of Ben More, but otherwise the group experienced good conditions overhead and underfoot. After a few brief stops on the route over A'Chioch the group reached the narrowing ridge leading to the summit. The cloud was now restricting visibility quite seriously, but in typical BSSMC style no one bothered to consult a map or compass. When it was felt that the summit was close, Andrew and Tom were ushered to the front of the group to lead the way up the final few hundred feet. They did manage to lose the route briefly, necessitating a short, steep scramble back up to the ridge to arrive at the summit, where Roderick and Karen had been freezing to death for about an hour waiting their arrival. The mist prevented any view at all but fortunately it did not bring any serious degree of precipitation with it. Champagne was opened and shared with a German couple who had reached the summit at the same time. "You do zees every time you climb a mountain in Scotland?" asked the bemused lady. She didn't really understand the complicated explanation which followed but she was happy to settle for more champagne. A fine buffet of fresh melon, oatcakes and pate, a celebratory cake and a bottle of Macallan was produced from Graham's extremely heavy rucksack, added to the supplies brought up by Rod and Karen and laid out on a tablecloth to complete the summit celebration.

While the party was going on, the sound of a light aircraft could be heard circling overhead but out of sight due to the mist. Graham revealed that Andrew's brother, Ian accompanied by his cousin, Alex Craig, had chartered a light aircraft and had flown from Glasgow Airport hoping to surprise the BSSMC on the summit with a flypast. Ian and Alex later reported that they had enjoyed excellent views all the way up to Mull and that the only cloud was sitting over Ben More, so the pilot had circled for a while before finally having to give up.

Two more climbers appeared at the summit cairn and joined the celebrations. One of them was about to complete his round of the Munros in a couple of weeks' time and took careful note of the proceedings. It was fairly chilly, so the party finished with a small dram and everyone set off down the gentle descent by the north west ridge to rejoin Audrey and Linda back at the cars.

Later that evening the group re-assembled at Macgochan's restaurant on Tobermory's new pier for a celebratory drink followed by an excellent meal in the small function room upstairs. A special menu had been agreed in advance with the restaurant. (see page 77)

After dinner "entertainment" was provided by Andrew and Tom, who spoke, fuelled by red wine and Macallan, of the many mountaineering friends who had helped make the BSSMC what it had become and delivered an illustrated history of people and events in its history. Tom also presented Andrew with a photographic record of the years they had spent together on the hills. Andrew and Tom then gave everyone present a specially printed BSSMC T-shirt and photos were taken of the group in club uniform. The evening ended with a ceremonial march along to the Post Office where Andrew and Tom posted off their application to "The Clerk of the List" to be officially recognised as having "compleated" the Munros.

It should be pointed out that at the 11th July 1997 there were 277 Munros. Andrew and Tom were well aware, however, that this was about to change with the publication, later in 1997, of a revised list of Munros which would increase the number to 284. They had been assured that, having completed the list as it was prior to publication of the revised list, their achievement would be recognised and that they need not feel obliged to rush out to climb any of the "new" Munros.

Over the next few days the various participants left to return home or to continue their holidays. The Vickerys and Sharpes stayed on for some gentle relaxation on Mull including a trip to Craignure to visit the Cathcarts for dinner in their caravan. On Sunday the 13th the Sharpes and Vickerys enjoyed a second celebratory dinner, much more sedate, at the Western Isles Hotel, the fine building which overlooks Tobermory Bay from the North. As they sailed back to Oban on the ferry next day they reflected quietly on the many happy years they had spent on the hills culminating in "compleation" as Munroists numbers 1769 and 1770.

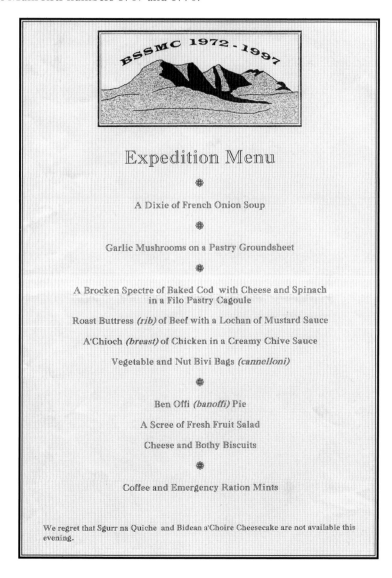

Chapter 22

Return to Torridon

The choice of venue for the 1998 annual expedition was, perhaps unsurprisingly, based on rather different criteria from the usual Munro led itinerary. Andrew and Tom suggested a trip to Torridon, for them a nostalgic return to the mountains of their youth. Alastair, Graham and Paul were happy to agree. Accommodation was arranged in Victoria Cottage, Shieldaig, one of the traditional, stone built houses facing the shore. It appeared to have been the home of an elderly gentleman, with some of his personal belongings, ornaments and furniture bringing an old fashioned and slightly sad atmosphere to the house. The old cake stand on the sideboard was put to good use – to hold the annual accounts. The cottage provided a comfortable and ideally located base for the week.

The journey north led to the usual stop in Fort William for lunch and supplies. On this occasion lunch was in the Ben Nevis bar –Alastair's preference as he knew that their mince and tatties didn't contain added vegetables, or "bits" which he continued to dislike. There was a shopping expedition to the Safeway in Fort William from where the receipt shows that the manager at that time was called Ronnie Corbett.

The week began with a full round of Beinn Alligin in good weather, beginning with the "Horns" and ending with a descent from Tom na Gruagach, down the badly eroded path through the corrie. Between them, Andrew and Tom had been on this mountain more often than any other, perhaps with the exception of Ben Lomond, so the day brought back many memories for them, including happy recollections of Dan Livingstone, whose ashes had been scattered near the top of Tom na Gruagaich following his death.

As an educational aside, a note about the scattering of ashes is included here. John Craig, one of those responsible for the scattering of Dan's ashes on Beinn Alligin, warns that anyone given this responsibility should take very careful note of the summit wind speed and direction before and during the actual event – for reasons which should be obvious but which may be overlooked in the emotion of the occasion.

The weather next day was overcast and quite cold, but dry, so the group elected to walk in towards Maol Chean-dearg. On the path above Loch an Eoin, the group split. Andrew and Tom wanted to climb An Ruadh Stac, one of the few hills (a Corbett rather than a Munro) in the area they had not been up, so they headed off to the summit. Alastair, Graham and Paul took the direct route to the summit of Maol Chean-dearg, before descending to the bealach and then climbing An Ruadh Stac, meeting Andrew and Tom on their way down. By this time low cloud and light rain had moved in and the huge quartzite blocks and slabs on An Ruadh Stac were becoming dangerously slippery.

Even after two fairly long days everyone was feeling good so the decision was taken to traverse Liathach from east to west. The path up from Glen Torridon had become something of a staircase, courtesy of Scottish National Trust path builders, since Andrew and Tom had last been on the hill many years before, so the summit ridge was reached fairly quickly. As a reminder that this was summer in Torridon, snow began to fall as the group arrived at Spidean a Choire Leith – big flakes which gave a brief white covering before melting to leave a wet, slippery surface on the quartzite blocks of that summit. The group traversed all the pinnacles successfully, Andrew and Tom feeling particularly pleased that they were still able to climb the final, exposed pinnacle without recourse to a rope (they didn't have one with them anyway). They were somewhat surprised that there was a very well marked route of descent to the glen, removing the need to consider the option of running the scree in the stone chute which had been the scene of the disintegration of Andrew's first boots many years before. On that occasion, having completed a traverse of Liathach, Andrew had been part of a group led by Jim Cathcart who, at the summit of Mullach an Rathan at 5pm, announced that he had arranged to collect ice-cream from the Post Office at Fasag, which closed at 5.30pm. Jim and Andrew set off down the stone chute at breakneck speed and entered the Post Office at 5.28pm. The descent by this new, eroded route was made at a far more leisurely pace.

A fine day on Bheinn Bhan followed, although Alastair decided to have a day off. Despite the high altitude start from the Bealach nam Bo, the group was reminded that this was not an "easy" hill, as they picked their way round the rough ground and crags to the summit plateau. Graham set off alone on a longer and more scenic descent while the others returned to the bealach, collecting Graham later.

Surprised by their overall levels of fitness and the continuing favourable weather, the group then took advantage of a warm, sunny day to climb Slioch. With terrific visibility, they were rewarded with magnificent views in all directions, able to see as far as Stornoway to the north-west.

Graham continued a real mountain marathon next day by going off on his own to climb Sgurr Ruadh and Beinn Liath Mhor while the others, beginning to feel the effects of their efforts so far, opted for a walk into Coire Mhich Fhearchar, with a view to climbing up the back of the corrie to Ruadh Stac Mor. Low cloud and light rain began to diminish enthusiasm for going beyond the corrie, a magnificent place in its own right anyway, and tiredness was also beginning to influence decision making. The group was happy to walk back down the Coire Dubh path.

Andrew recounted a story from one of his early visits to this area, of a very wet day in extremely poor visibility when he had been part of a group trying to locate the start of the Coire Dubh path from the lip of the corrie, as part of a group led by Dan, Jim Cathcart and the late Bob Campbell. Bob was a real mountaineer. He rarely needed to use a map or compass due to his knowledge of the area, he was an excellent rock climber who would often pause on a delicate stance to light a fag and ponder his next move, balancing on one foot as he concentrated on lighting up, he could keep going all day and was full of great stories. As the majority of those present that day in the rain began to conclude that they were well and truly lost, Bob pointed confidently and strode off on the line of his pointing finger, announcing that he could smell salt in the wind which was bringing the salt air up from Loch Torridon and all that was necessary was to keep smelling the air to remain on line. As everyone tried to follow his nasal navigation method, the line of the path eventually appeared before them and the clearing cloud confirmed they were where they should have been. Bob modestly acknowledged the adulation of the mountaineering novices in the group, which continued for the rest of the week, and his legendary status was assured. It was some years later, when being reminded of his unique skill, that he admitted he had known exactly where he was, having already seen the path close by and that he had simply made up the salty sign for fun.

In a week when most meals had been prepared at home in the cottage, it had been proving difficult to find a venue for the annual dinner. The Torridon Hotel (not the bar, which was far too rough for such a prestigious event) would have charged an amount roughly equivalent to the group budget for the week – well, nearly. Fortunately someone had spotted an advert for The Loch Kishorn Hotel and Seafood Restaurant so, on the Friday evening, with Alastair having kindly volunteered to be the driver, the group set off to find the hotel, having phoned ahead to reserve a table. They arrived to find, much to their surprise, a large, purpose built, modern bungalow with one large, open plan public room and a conservatory/dining room, open to non-residents. The quality of food was excellent, as was the standard of service provided by the lady owner, her sister and two young waitresses. The presence of these four young women and the close proximity of two fellow diners ensured that the standard of behaviour was somewhat better than was usual at a BSSMC dinner. The group needed little encouragement to sit in the lounge for after dinner drinks with pleasant music in the background. Conscious that Alastair had abstained from alcohol to be able to drive the others home, the group returned to Sheildaig, where Graham and Paul decided they just had time to squeeze in a nightcap in the pub, while their elders retired.

Graham and Paul were not seen again at Victoria Cottage until breakfast time next day, just in time to help with clearing up, packing and heading home. Both slept a lot on the return journey, complaining of being tired – certainly not hung-over. Between naps they recounted a tale of having been accosted outside the pub and encouraged into the back of a van by a couple who took them to their home on the outskirts of the village where they had plied the two reluctant prisoners with drink all night. During Graham and Paul's night time adventure the three elder statesmen had been sleeping soundly, exhausted by the week's efforts and dreaming of their younger days when they might have been able to cope with nightlife as well as days on the hill.

It had been a memorable return to Torridon.

Pinnacle on the ridge of Liathach

Chapter 23

……And Back to Onich

Preparatory discussions for 1999's annual expedition revolved round whether Andrew and Tom felt under any moral obligation to climb the "new" Munros which had been added during the recent revision to the list, at least the ones they had not already been up. Opinion was split, but as Graham had announced that there were some hills in the Glencoe area he had still to climb and there were some "new" Munros there too, a decision was made to head in that general direction.

Over the winter accommodation had been arranged through the Tourist Board in Fort William – Doraig Cottage in Onich. The owner was extremely difficult to pin down and even on the day of departure, Saturday 10th July, arrangements for entry remained vague. The journey north that day was notable for two reasons. Firstly Andrew, Alastair, Paul and Tom managed to make a significant contribution to global warming by taking three cars between them. Graham, however, had decided to cycle from Glasgow to Onich. By the time Andrew and Alastair arrived by car, Graham was already there, having covered the 100+ miles at an average speed of 18 miles per hour – a commendable effort. As they waited for the owner to arrive with the keys, Alastair discovered an unlocked sliding door (or forced open a sliding door, depending on how one interprets the amount of effort required to open it), much to Graham's relief as he was beginning to freeze to death in his sweaty lycra. After some re-arrangement of furniture in the kitchen and lounge to allow five seats to be placed permanently round the small dining table, Doraig Cottage served as a comfortable base for the week.

Mountaineering activity began next day with an enjoyable ascent of Buachaille Etive Beag, which took in one of the "new" summits missed by Andrew and Tom in 1981. The following day was undoubtedly the highlight of the week. Graham and Paul had never been along the Aonach Eagach and the others were happy to join them on this classic route again. The weather forecast was good, but the day started in low cloud. It was chilly as the group made its way up from the late Jimmy Savile's cottage, Allt-na-reigh, through swirling mist, with visibility just good enough to see where they were going. As they gained height, visibility began to improve gradually, offering promising glimpses of blue sky above and hints of views across the glen. Just below the ridge leading to Am Bodach, the group finally broke through the cloud to spectacular views across a mist filled Glencoe, to the high summits on the south side of the glen which were jutting through the carpet of low cloud. Above, there was clear blue sky and sunshine. Dragging themselves away from the spectacular views from Am Bodach, they set off along the ridge, mist still swirling below. Route finding along some of the trickier parts of the ridge prompted some discussion about whether Andrew and Tom had actually been here before. Any deviation from the route was attributed to old age and failing memory. Meanwhile, Alastair strode off in front, taking his usual direct route over anything in his way, regardless of difficulty, often a mile or so ahead of the others. As mist continued to bubble up from the corries to the north of the ridge, the group saw several Brocken Spectres and on one occasion Glories, where one's own shadow on the cloud below is encircled by a rainbow, one of the most spectacular sights one can witness on the hill. As the shadows waved back to their owners on the ridge, they strode on to re-join Alastair on Sgor nam Fiannaidh. A quick descent was made down the deep ruts of the badly eroded path to the Clachaig Inn where, celebrating a great day over welcome drinks at picnic tables, several low flying military aircraft supplied a fly past to complete a memorable day.

Sadly, the weather deteriorated next day as the group walked in to The Lost Valley, intending to climb Stob Coire Sgreamach, another of the "new" Munros. As the rain reached monsoon proportions the attempt on the summit was abandoned and the group paddled back to the cars in the glen. Paul had to leave for home that evening due to competing commitments.

Fortunately, better weather returned next day to allow an enjoyable traverse of all the tops of Buachaille Etive Mor, although it must be pointed out that only Graham visited the summit of Stob Dearg. Andrew and Tom were more interested in taking in the tops to the south to include Stob na Broige – guess what? - one of the "new" Munros!!

The bad weather returned next day to maintain its yo-yo pattern, but a decision was made to take a car across the Corran Ferry for a day on Garbh Bheinn, a Corbett often admired from the Ballachulish Bridge. On this particular day it remained invisible, hiding in low cloud. Parking the car in a lay-by, boots were pulled on but with little enthusiasm for an ascent. The still, damp conditions turned the bog by the lay-by into a midge sanctuary and it was probably the midge population which persuaded the reluctant climbers to set off up the hill, when it might have been wiser to get back into the car and head for indoor entertainment. Unfortunately, visibility was so poor that it was barely possibly to see the spectacular cliffs of the Great Ridge and the only thought was for getting back down after a very brief stop at the summit. The return journey via a path in the glen was of a sub-aqua nature and the welcoming committee of midges back at the car rounded off a thoroughly miserable day.

With clothes still drying from the previous day, there was no enthusiasm for a further soaking on the final day, which was also a bit damp, so the group elected for a general fester before the annual dinner in the restaurant which had opened some years earlier at Inchree, close enough to Doraig

Cottage to be able to walk there and back. Amazingly, there is a very good pavement all the way from the Corran Hotel to the Onich Hotel, which are roughly equidistant from Doraig Cottage, a pavement well used by BSSMC during the week.

It was so wet on the final Saturday that it took little persuasion for Graham to dismantle his bike and put it in the back of Andrew's car for the journey home. Maybe it was just as well they had brought so many cars after all.

Chapter 24

No Munros

Alastair had long been calling for some trips to hills which were not Munros and, at least since 1997, Andrew and Tom were beginning to warm to this idea. Finally in 2000 there was unanimity that the BSSMC would spend a week on the mountains of Assynt, where most of the hills are less than 3000 feet, with Ullapool being an ideal base. "Carnfune", a traditional cottage in the town, was the chosen base for this year's group of Alastair, Andrew, Graham, Paul and Tom.

The week began well with a successful rendezvous in Newtonmore, thanks in part to the first recorded use of mobile phones in BSSMC history – allowing contact to be maintained between the occupants of the two cars as they drove up the A9. Graham was delighted that his older companions had finally entered the 20th century, even although it was now the 21st. The two groups met for lunch in the Glen Hotel which had been the scene of the pilot BSSMC dinner in 1980. Andrew and Tom shuddered visibly at the sight of the Glenfarclas 105 behind the bar.

After lunch the group drove to Ullapool, arriving at the cottage slightly earlier than the agreed check-in time. Mrs. McKenzie, the owner, was still cleaning the cottage. On opening the door to the motley crew, she recalled that the let was to an all male group of 5 and said she had arranged to put an extra single bed in one of the rooms to allow every one a bed to themselves. In response to her question, "What do you usually drink with your meal in the evenings?" which aroused suspicions that she was discretely checking out whether this was the same group which had brought in crates of beer to "Bobby's" house in 1987, there was a very cautious response. It transpired that she didn't have any full sets of matching glasses in the cottage and an hour later, when the group returned from a brief walk to the shops, she had purchased two sets of glasses, for beer and wine, to make life a bit more comfortable. The cottage was very comfortable indeed, with one of the best equipped kitchens of all the cottages the BSSMC had rented, an important point as Tom liked to show off his considerable culinary skills and often bemoaned the lack of some gadget or other. The other rooms were comfortably furnished with old fashioned furniture which suited the cottage's traditional style. There was even a back garden with a small drying green and a bench outside the back door which was an ideal location for pre-prandial drinks (although the new glasses weren't taken outside).

The weather then made its contribution to a most enjoyable week. Apart from the Thursday, which was a day of blustery showers, allowing a general fester in and around Ullapool, the weather was quite settled. Each day was overcast but generally dry, cool and breezy, with occasional sunny spells to allow excellent views from the tops.

On Sunday the group enjoyed a walk over all the tops of Quinag. This was followed by a carefully planned day on Suilven. Using two cars, the group started off near Glencanisp Lodge at 10am for the long approach on good paths to the foot of the steep gully which offers easy access to the summit ridge from the north. The flat western top afforded magnificent views in all directions and a fine lunch spot, spoiled only by the totally inappropriate use of a mobile phone by one club member to share the moment with a colleague in Wales. The traverse of the summit ridge eastwards was interesting and involved a couple of entertaining scrambles. A long, curving descent to the north followed, with a good path being picked up for the long walk out to Inverkirkaig, where the other car had been left. On the walk out, everyone settled to their own pace, content to enjoy the beautiful late afternoon light, with magnificent scenery all around and particularly good views back to Suilven itself. Re-assembling at the car at 7pm, after a nine hour day, everyone agreed that this had been a particularly memorable day, which was then rounded off with a refreshment in "The Culag", the hotel on the pier which had become a base for the many eastern European and Russian fisherman who called in at Lochinver, hence its nickname "The Goulag" – not a place in which one would be tempted to linger. Times change, of course, and more recent reports suggest it is a much more welcoming place now.

After two quite long days, everyone was content to settle for a three hour scramble along Stac Pollaidh before another long day on Ben More Coigach. A close encounter with a pair of nesting red throated divers provided an enjoyable diversion on the walk in and the high winds on the summit were most entertaining, unless one happened to be trying to eat one's lunch.

With Thursday's blustery weather providing the ideal opportunity for a day of rest, afternoon tea for 5 was taken at a tearoom near Elphin at a total cost of £15.40. The English owner seemed keen to discourage potential customers by a series of notices containing the word "NO" – no smoking, no climbing boots, no wet clothes, no touching (of the stuffed animals), no large groups. A welcoming place?

The week was rounded off on Friday with a pleasant, easy day on Cul Mor allowing ample time to prepare for the annual BSSMC Dinner, to be held at the Ceilidh Place. Records show the total cost to have been £154.80, but there is no record of an annual argument or any outrageous behaviour. Surely the BSSMC wasn't becoming civilised?

With a fairly long journey home on Saturday, there was a final get together for lunch (again records are deficient in not recording the venue), where the accounts were finalised and debts settled. The total cost per person worked out at £183.83.

Chapter 25

Balnakyle 2001

At the closing meeting of the 2000 expedition a very loose arrangement had been made that the 2001 meeting would be held in Tomintoul, based at "Balnakyle," Jennifer Sharpe's family home which, Tom felt sure, could be rented for a nominal charge. One particular event over the winter, however, put the whole question of a 2001 expedition in jeopardy.

Not content with courting disaster by having pursued caving as a hobby, Tom had become enthusiastic about riding horses in recent years – another ridiculously dangerous pastime. Early in the winter he had had a riding accident. From his description of events the scenario bore some similarity to a horse riding stunt from a black and white Western. Riding along a country lane Tom's horse bolted, following the example of the horse in front. Unfortunately, the full width of the road was occupied by a Volvo estate car (were there cars in black and white Westerns or did they appear later?). As the horses squeezed past on either side of the car, flailing limbs, stirrups and other bits systematically took out both headlamps, both wing mirrors, the windscreen and the aerial of the Volvo. At some point Tom's jacket caught in the hawthorn hedge at the side of the lane and he was dislodged from his mount, landing on his head on the road. Unfortunately his left foot remained caught in the stirrup and Tom was dragged, fortunately unconscious, along the lane until an ankle bone broke and his foot fell from the stirrup. Eventually, when the horse came to a stop, it was evident that Tom had been seriously injured. He suffered a broken ankle and torn ankle ligaments and ended up seriously plastered. He was determined not to miss a BSSMC expedition, however, and being based at Balnakyle at least offered him some home comforts while the others ventured out on the hill.

So on Sunday 1st July, still using a crutch to get about, Tom met up with Alastair, Andrew and Graham at Balnakyle, having endured an uncomfortable journey from Cardiff. His participation in the week was largely confined to cooking for the group and limping with them to the pub (his limp seemed less pronounced on the return journeys), but he made every effort to support the week's activities. To add to the team's injury list, Paul was suffering severe pain in one knee, a recurring problem probably caused by his unhealthy interest in throwing himself downhill on a plank, or snowboarding as he called it. He joined the group on the Tuesday evening.

With Andrew and Tom having completed the Munros, it was now usually left to Graham to decide which hills he wanted to climb – he was being given every encouragement to finish off the Munros himself, the others being keen to arrange a celebratory party. So on Monday, Alastair, Andrew and Graham drove round to the A9 for an ascent of Meall Chuaich. Tom stayed behind and prepared dinner for their return. The mountaineering trio repeated the journey next day, this time driving to the top of Glen Feshie for a day on the two Munros there, a sad comedown from the last time Andrew had been there with Tom in 1981, when the same range of hills had offered five Munros. On this occasion Andrew was content to accompany the others to the summit of Carn Ban Mor before watching them race off to take in the other summit.

With Paul having arrived on the Tuesday night, Andrew elected to have the next day off to keep Tom company, while Alastair, Graham and Paul planned a rather complicated expedition. The idea was that Graham and Paul would drive round to the Linn O'Dee, from where they would climb all the summits south of Braeriach. Meanwhile, Alastair wanted to walk through the Lairig Ghru from north to south, meeting the other two at Linn O' Dee for the return journey to Tomintoul. So, Graham and Paul set off early while Andrew and Tom gave Alastair a lift to the start of the Lairig Ghru path at Loch Morlich. Andrew and Tom then went off for a short walk round Loch an Eilein, quite an effort for Tom, followed by a bar lunch in Aviemore and assorted touristy activities, oblivious of developments on the hill.

Having made rapid progress through the first half of the Lairig Ghru, Alastair deviated from his plan and decided to take in Ben Macdui en route. Still well ahead of schedule he arrived at the Linn O' Dee far too early to meet the others, so he left a note on the car windscreen and walked round to the pub in Braemar. Meanwhile, having reached the Devil's Point, Paul's knee had given out and he felt unable to carry on with Graham. He set off on his own to return, slowly, to the car, while Graham carried on alone to complete the five summits of the plateau before returning to Linn O'Dee.

Graham and Paul met up at the car, but there was no sign of Alastair, which surprised them as it was getting late in the day. They didn't see Alastair's note – he had put it on the wrong car! Paul tried to phone Tomintoul but couldn't get through, so he phoned Charley, his partner, in Edinburgh who, in turn, phoned Tomintoul to inform Tom of the developing situation. Tom then phoned Alastair on his mobile phone to discover he was sitting in the pub in Braemar, surprised that Graham and Paul hadn't joined him by now. Another relay of phone calls ended with the three wandered souls finally re-uniting for a bar meal in Braemar, being too late to get back in Tomintoul for dinner. Meanwhile, Andrew and Tom were nursing their wrath in Balnakyle, eating dinner for five and awaiting the safe but late return of their friends. Once again, the BSSMC had failed completely to recognise its inability to cope with complicated logistics and that mobile phones could not be relied on in mountainous areas. Poor Alastair was berated for his un-announced change of route. His defence of having been travelling the hills

Celebrating Compleation on Ben More

Clearing skies in Glencoe

Andrew on The Cantilever, Glyder Fach, Snowdonia

The Devil's Kitchen, Cwm Idwal, Snowdonia

The Summit of Tryfan - Adam and Eve

BSSMC at Corrour Station

Loch Quoich from Gleouraich

The Forcan Ridge on The Saddle

alone for the best part of twenty five years and therefore not being used to tight arrangements was dismissed as "irresponsible" by the others who were, of course, completely responsible at all times!

Although the weather next day was reasonable, everyone felt in need of a rest day after Paul's injury, Graham's marathon and Alastair's mystery tour the previous day. Andrew had brought his fishing rod with him, having taken up fly fishing fairly recently, and decided that this was the day when fishing should be introduced as a BSSMC activity. No one else was interested in keeping him company so he spent a very pleasant day on the River Avon alone, apart from occasional encounters with one or two embarrassingly small trout. Meanwhile the others took in the delights of local tourist attractions, coffee shops and pubs. They all met up for dinner, disappointed that Andrew had not returned with ingredients for the main course.

Sgurr an Lochain Uaine was one of the "new" Munros which Andrew and Tom had not been up, having deliberately contoured round its then non-Munro summit in 1986. While Tom was content to have completed the "old" Munros, Andrew felt some sort of moral obligation to visit the summits he had not been up. For a long time he had wanted to visit Glen Einich and the others were happy to join him on this route to Sgurr an Lochain Uaine. Alastair, Andrew, Graham and Paul set off from the small parking area at the end of the public road, keeping up a fast pace for the long walk in to Loch Einich. Here, Paul decided his knee was not up to the strenuous climb ahead and opted to walk back slowly to the car. The remaining three made good progress up a stalker's path into low cloud and drizzle as they neared the plateau below the summit. At this point, Alastair's response to the moist conditions was to strip down to running shorts and vest, based on his theory that human skin is the best water resistant material available, far better than any synthetic fabric which should be removed as far as possible. It was evident from the backward glances of passing walkers that they did not appreciate Alastair's theory, which proved sound apart from the two occasions when the group stopped to eat and he nearly froze to death. The group returned via Braeriach and the Lairig Ghru, a trip of 21miles and 5½ thousand feet of ascent.

The weather on Saturday was poor, so everyone was content to have another festering day. Tomintoul offered minimal choice when it came to selecting a venue for the annual BSSMC dinner. The lounge bar of the Gordon Hotel proved to be a good choice, however. The food was excellent, but credit for creating a good atmosphere must go to a salmon fishing group from south of the border, who drowned out the comparatively quiet BSSMC. Musical entertainment was provided by an elderly gentleman who played the accordion. He was happy to play requests and responded to the BSSMC's "deedle-e-dee" rendition of the theme tune to "Captain Pugwash" by playing the melody, while the BSSMC sang the "deedle-e-dee" lyrics and drummed on the table. Some years later it was discovered that this tune is actually entitled "Trumpet Hornpipe". Over a number of years it had become the unofficial BSSMC theme tune (to be noted when a film is being considered).

Leaving Tomintoul on the Sunday, Andrew and Graham had a rather wet 4¾ hour trip round the A9 tops of Carn na Caim and A'Bhuidheanach Beag, with Graham demonstrating considerable skill with map and compass in amongst the peat hags. Meanwhile Alastair and Tom had gone off to visit geological sites (not the parallel roads of Glenroy, for a change). The two groups met up at 7pm for a bar meal in Comrie, bringing the 2001 meeting to a close.

Chapter 26

North Wales

At the conclusion of the 2001 meeting the suggestion had been made that the mountains of North Wales would make an interesting venue for the 2002 expedition. By the beginning of winter this continued to seem like a good idea for a number of reasons; as Tom had still not recovered fully from his injury, there was some doubt as to whether he would be able to manage a full week away and if he had to return home it would be a shorter journey than from Scotland. He also had a good knowledge of these hills from many previous visits so it seemed reasonable that the Scottish residents should travel south for a change.

However, as winter passed into spring, organising the trip was becoming increasingly difficult. Tom was commuting to Newfoundland, finalising a work related project which was running to a very vague schedule. As Tom was the main man on this project, making any forward plan for his summer holiday was difficult for him. But the final straw was the temporary disappearance of Tom's personal organiser (a diary, not a person), which threw his ability to make any firm commitment out of the window. Its loss began to take on the proportions of "Wee Annie's Red Yo-Yo" from the Matt McGinn song, with the police being informed at one stage as the international crisis grew. The poor organiser, however, was simply seeking temporary respite by hiding under the front seat of Tom's car – who would have thought of checking there?!!

Finally, in late June arrangements were put in place but, by this time, neither Alastair nor Paul was available, so only Andrew and Graham drove south on Sunday 14th July to rendezvous with Tom at Capel Curig Youth Hostel.

The hostel was a rather dilapidated building externally, in need of some maintenance, but it was comfortable and homely inside – and very busy all week. At this time of year in that area it was almost inevitable that one semi-permanent resident was a geology student engaged on her mapping project. Some other fellow hostellers were interesting to observe. There was a group of noisy and extremely untidy schoolboys from Manchester, who appeared to hold the collective view that the purpose of toilet paper was to act as wall to wall carpeting. Their teachers spared other hostellers further disturbance by making the youngsters cook and eat outside on a makeshift barbecue. Then there was a group of Japanese young people of varying ages who arrived very late one evening but who, despite obvious exhaustion, behaved impeccably as they waited to be allocated rooms. Over the next few days much bowing took place as good manners prevailed in the hostel. Doors were held open and there was much "giving way" to anyone coming up a flight of stairs, accompanied by more bowing, of course.

A further memorable aspect of the hostel was that it operated on a Bed and Breakfast basis, with no option other than to join the queue to indulge in the full cooked breakfast which gave a considerable boost to group cholesterol levels over the week. The Japanese, who queued in small groups as directed by their leader, sat silently as they ate the less cholesterol intensive items from the breakfast buffet.

A fairly settled spell of weather gave dry, pleasantly warm conditions, with occasional low cloud and haze, allowing five consecutive days on the hill during which the 14 Welsh 3000ft summits were climbed. Andrew and Graham had made the reasonable assumption that Tom's previous experience of these mountains would prove useful when it came to route finding. Tom's oft repeated excuse of "it's a long time since I was here" seemed feeble, particularly when, in front of a large audience, he led the group off the sheer face of Snowdon while attempting the descent to Lliwedd. His route finding on the ascent of Tryfan and the Bristly Ridge was equally interesting, leading to places where the rule of thumb became – maintain eight points of contact with the rock at all times unless jumping.

The first hills of the week were Y Garn and Elidir Fawr via The Devil's Kitchen, an enjoyable introduction to the impressive northern end of the Glyders. Andrew and Graham were impressed by the well constructed paths and stone staircases through the cliffs and soon became aware that with very little soft ground underfoot there was going to be much wear and tear on the soles of the feet this week. Records show that this trip took 6hrs 40mins.

Just to allow the introduction of more Welsh place names, it should be noted that the next day was spent on Pen Yr Ole-Wen, by a relentless slog straight up from Idwal, on to Carnedd Dafydd and Carnedd Llewelyn by the pleasant going of the Carneddau ridge – another fine 6hr 30min day.

Wednesday and Thursday brought the main events of the week. First, the ascent of Snowdon, beginning with the enjoyable, exposed scramble along Crib Goch, where the Scottish contingent found the queuing system, as large numbers of groups took it in turn to traverse narrow sections of the ridge, a somewhat alien mountain procedure, but necessary. As mist closed in, they reached the summit, Yr Wyddfa, coinciding with the arrival of one of the "trains" on the mountain railway from Llanberis, which disgorged vast numbers of tourists into the summit café. Given the cold, damp mist outside, the BSSMC took little persuading to join the queue of tourists for a hot drink in the café. The scene at the summit cairn was surreal – climbers and hillwalkers, suitably dressed for the conditions, mixed with tourists of every age who were dressed in clothes more suited to the beach or the shops they had left behind in Llanberis than the mist shrouded summit at 3560 feet. Perhaps it was desperation to escape this place which led to Tom's dodgy route finding, but it wasn't long until they were back on track to complete the round of the horseshoe on Lliwedd Bach.

In better visibility the group enjoyed a long stop on Lliwedd Bach, observing a small helicopter hovering at the base of the steep slopes of Crib Goch opposite. They could see what looked like mountain rescue team members, in no particular hurry, coming and going from the helicopter to the steep screes above, presumably a training exercise. Returning to the car at Pen-y-pass their arrival coincided with that of a Sea King helicopter, for which an area of the car park had been cleared to allow it to land. As it hovered above the parked cars, items of mountaineering equipment were ripped from open car boots and half eaten sandwiches were blown away from surprised diners, by the incredible downdraught from the huge rotors. The occupants of the helicopter were the R.A.F mountain rescue team members returning from the retrieval of a dead body – someone who had fallen from Crib Goch, almost certainly someone who had been in the queue with the BSSMC earlier in the day.

With the north ridge being the classic route of ascent to the summit of Tryfan, it was the route chosen by the BSSMC on Thursday. The rough scree paths through boulders and heather at the start of the route dampened enthusiasm, but they were soon on to scrambling on good rock, becoming increasingly exposed as the ridge narrowed towards the summit. The highest points at the summit of Tryfan are two eight feet tall blocks of rock known as "Adam and Eve". Graham led the way up the narrower of the two blocks before jumping across the gap to the other – the gap being just too wide to permit stepping across, then jumping back. Andrew followed, then Graham was sent up again by Tom to allow him to use the video facility on his fairly new digital camera. Due to Tom's unfamiliarity with the operation of the video function, Graham had to make the jump several times before his leap was captured for posterity.

The aptly named Bristly Ridge, the continuation of the route from Tryfan to Glyder Fach, offered a series of increasingly exposed scrambles up several rock towers and narrow ledges through notches between the towers. While guide books describe this route as "entertaining", it was soon evident that two members of the BSSMC had outgrown this sort of entertainment as they clung on by fingernails in places they probably should not have been. The group was relieved to reach the summit of Glyder Fach, featuring a huge slab of rock, known as "The Cantilever", which juts out for about 10 feet beyond a rock fulcrum on which it is perfectly balanced. The route across to the next summit of the Glyders, Glyder Fawr, crossed a plateau of huge boulders and angled slabs of rock which point skywards. Finding these slabs awkward to walk across, Graham opted to run, leaping from one sharp edge to the next. Moving at some speed, he missed his footing on one slab and took off into mid air, with Andrew and

Tom holding their breaths as his horizontal body headed towards the very sharp edge of the next jutting rock. He was heading for at least a broken arm - and another close encounter with a Sea King Helicopter seemed inevitable, but at the last minute he twisted himself in mid-air to engineer a pretty painful bounce on to a flatter surface nearby.

On the final uneventful stages of the descent from the Glyders the BSSCMC group was questioned by a mountain rescue team member who was trying to locate a climber, reportedly injured after a fall. By a process of elimination he had worked out a likely location and made a radio call for a helicopter. The yellow Sea King was overhead in minutes and by the time the group had changed clothes at the car near Idwal Hostel, the injured climber had been airlifted to the roadside and transferred to a waiting ambulance.

The group had to stay at Idwal hostel that night as the hostel at Capel Curig had been pre-booked to capacity, probably offering the Japanese group ample opportunity to engage in much door holding and bowing. Idwal was full too and one long distance walker was caught out with no-where to stay – the hostel warden being unreasonably inflexible. Having witnessed his rejection, the BSSMC was moved to offer assistance. Tom borrowed Andrew's car to drive the stranded walker to Capel Curig where he would at least have a choice of Bed and Breakfast accommodation.

By Friday the weather was beginning to deteriorate. By the time the BSSMC had made the long drive to the valley of Afon Llafar for an ascent of the northern summit of the Carneddau, it seemed likely they were going to get wet for the first time that week. The rain held off for the walk in and the ascent of Foel Grach and for the walk out to Yr Elen and back before finally setting in as the group walked out to the final 3000ft summit, Foel-fras. The sense of achievement on having completed all the Welsh 3000 footers in a week was somewhat diminished by an encounter with a young man on the summit of Foel-fras, who was also just finishing the same round of hills, but he had done so inside 24 hours. The long walk back to the car was completed in increasingly heavy rain, but the feeling of satisfaction at having completed the Welsh "Munros" outweighed the misery of a soaking.

The annual BSSMC dinner was held that evening in the comfortable bar of the Bryn Twrch hotel, an up market and most enjoyable bar meal. Interestingly, Graham didn't have scampi, he had a vegetable samosa, followed by a Thai curry and he drank Hoegaarden beer at £3 a bottle.

The next morning was wet, but Tom seemed determined that the week should end with an ascent of the hill directly opposite the hostel, Moel Siabod, which, he assured the others, was a very nice hill. Well, it might be in decent weather but on a wet July Saturday it was pretty miserable. The rocky ridge to the summit was very slippery and the rock was cold and wet to the touch. The very wet ascent was followed by an even wetter descent, during which the group encountered a group of, presumably mad, fell runners, racing up the hill in shorts and running vests. Thoughts turned to the absent Alastair. Fortunately the misery of the day lasted only 3½ hours. To compensate, the group enjoyed a second annual dinner, this time in the Tyn-y-Coed Hotel down the road from the hostel. This was a fine conclusion to a very enjoyable, successful and eventful week. Tom's ankle had held up well and he had enjoyed re-visiting the hills of his youth, even if he seemed not to remember them terribly well. The others had enjoyed the trip abroad and had been very impressed by the magnificent mountains of North Wales.

Bristly Ridge, Tryfan, Snowdonia

Chapter 27

The 25th Annual Meeting

The BSSMC founder members were aware that 2003 would be the 25th consecutive year in which they had had at least one annual expedition together, along with a varying number of companions. In planning the 2003 meeting they tried to find a central venue to make it as easy as possible for any occasional participants to join them, even for a day or so, to help celebrate such an auspicious occasion. They were also alert to their need to continue encouraging Graham towards "compleation", so wanted to be near some hills he hadn't been up. Graham himself was less troubled by this particular criterion.

A fairly recent development of new lodges and renovated cottages at Portnellan, just outside Crianlarich, had been identified as an ideal location. Ardencaple Cottage was being upgraded early in 2003 and was available for a very reasonable £342. Coincidentally, it was very close to the exact spot where Tom and Andrew had first met in 1972 to climb Ben More. Other BSSMC members were completely un-moved by such nostalgia and invited guests had better things to do in July, so it was left to the stalwarts of the BSSMC - Alastair, Andrew, Graham, Paul, Roderick and Tom – to form the expedition force for this significant anniversary.

Travel arrangements to the venue were complicated from the outset. On the Saturday evening Alastair and Tom had been invited by Mike McGinnes to his house warming party – a barbecue – at his new home in Kinnesswood. By coincidence the house turned out to be almost directly opposite where Stuart MacKenzie, Roderick's brother, had been living for many years. Stuart and his wife, Jacqui, had been invited to the party by the new neighbours who were unaware of Stuart's connection to the BSSMC. As well as being Roderick's brother, Stuart had been an Inveralligin stalwart and had been part of the group described in Chapter 1.

It is perhaps worth devoting a few paragraphs to how travel arrangements unfolded, if only to illustrate how complicated it had become trying to assemble BSSMC members in one place at the same time. On the Friday evening Roderick had driven up from Manchester to stay overnight with Andrew in Peebles. They spent some time on Saturday morning buying and preparing food, then Roderick drove off to Kinnesswood to visit Stuart, before going with him to Mike's party. Meanwhile, Tom had flown from Cardiff to Prestwick on the Friday to visit his dad in Ayr, from where Alastair picked him up by car. They set off for Kinnesswood, arranging a rendezvous with Andrew in Callander in mid-afternoon. Andrew drove north with a car load of food for the Callander rendezvous. Graham was travelling independently from Glasgow. His plan was to take his bike in his car, have a cycle run in Glen Lyon before meeting Andrew and Paul at Crianlarich. Paul wanted to take his own car to Crianlarich because – and this is a long, but relevant, story – his partner, Charley Malalieu, was visiting Killin that week with her mother to help clear the house where her grandfather, who had died recently, had lived for many years. The house was now for sale. Paul wanted to be able to drive round to Killin some evenings to visit so wanted his own car. It was therefore anyone's guess where and when they might all meet up.

Andrew, Alastair and Tom did manage to meet up in Callander, thanks to the assistance of good old mobile phones which by now had become indispensable pieces of mountaineering equipment. Some beer, wine and even bubbly to help celebrate the occasion of the 25th meeting was purchased then Andrew drove on to Crianlarich, leaving Alastair and Tom to head straight to the Kinnesswood party. Paul was at Ardencaple Cottage by the time Andrew arrived. They unpacked the food and allocated bedrooms in the absence of the others. They were relieved to see that the upgrading was more or less complete and the standard of furniture and fittings would ensure a comfortable week. Fortunately, there was an adequate number of electric sockets, an absolute necessity to accommodate the growing array of computers and electronic gadgetry which now accompanied BSSMC members. Meanwhile, Graham had reported in that he was behind schedule as his cycle ride had taken longer than planned. Finally he arrived much later than scheduled, unloaded, washed and changed before he, Paul and Andrew drove to Kinnesswood to join the party.

Meanwhile at Kinnesswood, Alastair and Tom had arrived while Roderick, Stuart and Jacqui had walked across the road to meet the new neighbours and make introductions, before the trio from Crianlarich arrived to complete the group. In between conducted tours of his new home Mike, who had clearly been enjoying a refreshment or two, was in charge of the barbecue. Without wishing to cast aspersions on his culinary skills, it can only be said that much of the barbecued food was, well, rather rare. The accompanying salad dishes were, however, devoured by the starving BSSMC members. Finally, with darkness falling, the BSSMC set off for base camp. Unable to wait for the annual dinner to have the annual argument, Alastair and Graham engaged in a very long debate en route. Given the hectic start to the week, there was general agreement that the next day should be an easy one.

Beinn Challum was the chosen hill for the first day. The early stages of the route involved following the West Highland Way for a short stretch. Presumably for the benefit of W.H.W walkers, an information board about Saint Fillan had been erected at the side of the path near St.Fillan's chapel. The group was astonished and somewhat disturbed to note that the illustration of Saint Fillan bore more than a passing resemblance to Mike McGinnes. Anyone who knows Mike may wish to check out the amazing similarity for themselves. The summit was reached in deteriorating visibility as light rain began. Andrew and Tom were rather disappointed that the summit cairn bore no trace of a large wooden fence pole they had built into the cairn sometime in the 1970s, the transportation of which had caused terminal damage to a rucksack of Tom's.

Returning to Ardencaple Cottage fairly early, the bubbly was opened to mark the official celebration of the 25th Annual Meeting of the BSSMC (pedants may require the explanation that there were two years in which two expeditions took place and that the event being celebrated was therefore really the 25th consecutive year of annual meetings and also that it was not actually the 25th anniversary of the first meeting). Andrew supplied a light buffet of his home smoked trout and trout pate, in an attempt to support the fact he had again brought fishing rods with him and was clearly putting down a marker for introducing less strenuous activities into the week. Some early drafts of chapters from this book were produced for entertainment but this merely hastened an end to the early evening celebrations which then moved on to an excellent dinner.

Despite two consecutive evenings partying, the group was up very early next morning to catch the early morning train from Crianlarich to Corrour, for the ascent of Carn Dearg and Sgorr Gaibhre. Alastair and Graham raced off to take in Beinn na Lap (no doubt Alastair wanted to check that his 1983 snow patch was still there) while the others opted for a more gentle return down the loch side, stopping to look at the controversial new lodge being built at the head of the loch for Lisbet Rausing, heiress to the £6 billion TetraPak fortune. The full group re-assembled at Corrour station, for tea and cakes in the recently opened bunkhouse/café (controversially closed by the estate in late 2004 then later re-opened), before catching the late afternoon train back to Crianlarich.

The weather broke next day, with strong winds and rain, so a day of festering was declared. Andrew and Paul took one of the estate's boats to fish on Loch Dochard, with no success, although they did have a close encounter with a huge salmon (honestly!). In the evening Paul drove round to Killin to meet Charley and her mum, returning with an invitation for the group to make use of the swimming pool at the house. An outdoor pool, in Killin, with midges! The invitation was greeted with muted enthusiasm. Meanwhile, arrangements had been made to meet Stuart MacKenzie next day for a visit to two of the outlying tops of Ben Lawers.

Fortunately, Wednesday brought better weather, with some hazy sunshine. The group of six met Stuart in the car park at Ben Lawers and enjoyed a pleasant day on the two "Meall"s which form the high ridge running north to Glen Lyon. Leaving Stuart to return home, the others, still not convinced by Paul's re-assurance that he had turned up the thermostat on the heating for the swimming pool, drove to Dochart House in Killin, where they were welcomed by Charley and her mum in the kitchen, which was big enough to accommodate two large dining tables. Over a few beers, the group heard a brief history of the house. On his retiral from his position as the last Queen's Commissioner in Bechuanaland (which became Botswana), Charley's grandfather, Sir Peter Fawcus, had purchased and improved the house, developing the extensive grounds. He had incorporated a heated, kidney shaped swimming pool into the walled garden. The house itself contained many souvenirs and gifts from his days as a senior diplomat in Africa. The swimming pool had been the one and only pool in Killin and over many years had been used by young school children from the village, who had always been made welcome at the house.

The group was invited out to the pool, where Charley's mum had laid out a trolley loaded with snacks and more beer. Paul led the way into the pool, through a fine, floating layer of dead midges. Alastair and Graham soon joined him, while Andrew contented himself with the task of clearing dead midges from the surface with a large net – his best catch of the week. Tom delighted in taking photos of the rather surreal scene, while Roderick lay back and enjoyed the view of Meall nan Tarmachan from the sheltered garden. As the enjoyable evening wore on Charley's mum announced that people were due to be viewing the house, which was by now for sale. The BSSMC members offered to leave, but were encouraged to stay as "so many people enjoying themselves by the pool makes the place looks lived in." More beer led to an agreement that the BSSMC would purchase a lottery ticket for the coming weekend and when they won the jackpot would buy the house as a permanent headquarters. Needless to say, the win did not materialise.

The weather deteriorated next day so a further fester was deemed in order. The area around Crianlarich has little entertainment to offer on a wet day and no one has much recollection of how they passed the day. However, the annual accounts show that lunch was taken at Struie Lodge, which was going through one of its many re-births.

Friday's weather wasn't much better, but the group drove to Glencoe with the intention of climbing Stob Coire Sgreamach, one of Andrew and Tom's outstanding "new Munros". After an hour or so sitting in cars with condensed windows, occasionally opening them to check on the levels of precipitation, everyone apart from Alastair set off in fine drizzle, having convinced one another the rain was easing. The Lost Valley was as impressive as ever, the mist and flooded river adding to the atmosphere of isolation and mystery. A new path had been built towards the bealach below Sgreamach. It eventually deteriorated at the base of a very wet and loose scree slope. Roderick opted to return to the cars while the others carried on to the summit, pausing for just a few minutes and returning as quickly as possible by the same route.

The day had been particularly significant for Andrew as this was the last of the "new Munros" he hadn't been up before – a matter of honour!

The annual dinner in the Falls of Dochart Inn in Killin that evening was particularly enjoyable. The atmosphere was good and the food was excellent. After dinner, Charley, her mother and a friend joined the group for drinks, unwittingly preventing the annual BSSMC argument from breaking out. Charley's mum and her friend seemed to be taking something of a shine to Alastair but they were left in no doubt that Alastair's services as driver (a double run to Crianlarich) were required by the other BSSMC members so they could just leave him alone. Alastair's service as chauffeur to the BSSMC was recognised in the shape of a special "drinks adjustment" to his final bill for the week.

Despite the poor weather it had been a very good week. The 25th annual meeting was brought to a close formally on the Saturday morning, the total bill for the week, £920.08, being divided up and debts settled before everyone went their separate way, agreeing to meet again for the 26th annual meeting in 2004.

Chapter 28

Na Tighean Beaga Revisited

The quest for the completion of the Munros by Graham had, by now, become a priority, although more in the minds of Andrew and Tom than in Graham's, probably because of their advancing years and their desire for a party while they would still be able to enjoy it. After a winter of Graham compiling a "still to do" list it was agreed that the Spean Bridge area would offer maximum opportunity to get more ticks on it. A booking was made for one of the larger chalets at Na Tighean Beaga, where the group had stayed in 1993.

For the second successive year, Tom's travel plans had been influenced by the availability of cheap flights from Cardiff, and with Paul having to delay joining the others because he was going to a wedding, only Andrew's car was available for the trip north, so arrangements were complicated – again!

Tom flew from Cardiff to Edinburgh at an unhealthily early hour where Andrew, astonished by Tom's frugality in terms of luggage, met him. They drove to Glasgow to collect Graham, fairly sedately in order not to arouse him from his slumbers. Having managed to get all the luggage in the boot, a decision was made over coffee (read Coke in relation to Graham) at Inverarnan, that lunch would be taken at Fort William followed by a BSSMC shopping expedition. Lunch was, of course, taken at the West End Hotel and Safeway was the venue for the purchase of £140.28's worth of supplies. The term food cannot be applied in the strictest sense as almost one third of the bill was for alcoholic beverages. For the few remaining miles to Roy Bridge, Graham was hidden under a sea of Safeway bags and cardboard boxes on the rear seat.

The chalet was a large one, capable of sleeping 8, booked using the logic that if Alastair, whose schedule was always difficult to predict accurately, appeared there would be five in the group and a chalet for eight would be more acceptable than one for four. As things turned out, for the first two nights there were only three, allowing the luxury of a room each. As a lengthy unpacking exercise took place and food was finding its way into cupboards and a rather undersized fridge, there was an amazing discussion about how best to ensure the fresh basil retained its freshness, for use later in the week; keep it in the fridge, wrapped, unwrapped, frozen or just in its sealed bag? Changed days, indeed, from the days of the Knoydart Rations and packets of dried food.

Eventually thoughts turned to getting out on to some mountains and with a weather forecast suggesting that rain would never be far away, it was decided that Sunday would be used for the nearby hills of Stob Coire Sgriodan and Chno Dearg. The weather forecast was correct and it was a rather dreich day. The highlight was, undoubtedly, the observation and discussion of fluvial bifurcation and even trifurcation at one point, spotted earlier on the map by one of the non-geologists in the group, but identified on location by the one who was qualified to speak on the subject. The level of excitement was tangible and there was clear reluctance to leave the site for the wet plod back to the car. For the benefit of any reader wishing to observe this location personally, it is at grid reference 361763 and several points nearby, on OS sheet 41. Further information can, of course, be obtained from T. Sharpe.....

Monday 5th July 2004 was one of those less enjoyable days on the hill, saved only by the series of side visits along the way. With a forecast suggesting that the marginally less bad weather would be west of the Great Glen, a decision was made to climb Gairich. The day began well enough with an enjoyable drive to the Tomdoun Hotel for coffee. The hotel evoked memories for Andrew and Tom as they bored Graham with descriptions of how the interior had changed over 25 years. Moving on towards the dam at Loch Quoich, Andrew and Tom identified the spot where they had camped in 1979 on their retreat from Knoydart so they stopped to take photographs – a poignant moment. As they left the car, walked across the dam and started round the loch on a very wet and boggy path it was dry – for ten minutes. From then the day went downhill as the group pondered the wisdom of going uphill. The path was a quagmire at its good bits, a muddy burn with tempting pockets of deep mud for most of the way and it seemed much longer than Andrew and Tom remembered. After passing through a huge group of young people camping in the boggiest, most midge ridden place imaginable, the trio struck up an even wetter, boggier path leading up hill. Despite its gradient there was no let up in the mud. As Graham strode off into the distance across a flatter, boggy expanse on the shoulder of the ridge, Tom, whose knee was beginning to complain, elected to return to the car. Andrew pressed on to join Graham on the now badly eroded, muddy steep section, in showery weather. Only for a couple of hundred feet were underfoot conditions reasonable. A few brief clear spells allowed decent views eastwards from the summit, a long, low rainbow adding some colour to the otherwise drab scene. With little to encourage a long stay at the top, the pair beat a hasty retreat across the varying degrees of bog. The puddles on the final stretches of "path" near the loch were capable of swallowing most things on two legs given half a chance and the rain eased only enough to ensure that wet clothes which were removed had to be put back on minutes later. Resisting the temptation to bury a bad day over a few drinks at the Tomdoun Hotel, the group sped back to Roy Bridge, where Paul, who had recently arrived, was waiting. Of course, for Paul's benefit, the story was one of a great hill, sunshine and superb views. Only the pile of wet clothes and muddy boots suggested otherwise.

Fortunately, the next day brought better weather, so the group set off for Creag Meagaidh, opting for the route up Coire Ardair to the "window", the same route as had been taken in 1984. As the path steepened over the final few hundred feet, it was evident to those behind that Graham had put his foot on the accelerator and that his turbo charger was fully functional. That was the cue for the group to split. Graham and Paul pressed on to the summit, returned to the window and completed the Munros to the north of Coire Ardair, while Andrew and Tom contented themselves with a more leisurely ascent, taking time to enjoy the summit and returning by the path down Coire Ardair. Showers had made the railway sleepers, from which long sections of the path were constructed, very slippery and Tom enjoyed a free white knuckle ride on his back, sliding for some distance down a section of sleepers, water spraying off to the side.

Wednesday's weather forecast suggested hills to the west would be the best option – the central location of Roy Bridge makes it ideal when there is an east/west, or indeed north/south split in the weather– so the group headed for the two Munros to the west of Loch Lochy. The chosen route began at Kilfinnan providing the opportunity for a car to be taken as close to the hill as possible. The path to the bealach between the two summits enabled good progress to be made, delays being caused only by a series of calls to and from Tom's mobile phone regarding major cock-ups at work, which he was finding impossible to leave behind. First fresh basil, now work issues by phone on the hill, what would be next? These hills afford great views up and down the Great Glen, particularly on the descent to the north. The weather remained dry and bright, but clearly was being less kind to hills in most other directions.

The one difficulty with the chosen descent route, apart from a high degree of steepnitude through a band of cliffs, is the need to negotiate some bracken clad slopes close to the forestry road above the loch. In places the bracken was shoulder high and the terrain underfoot was often invisible. Suddenly Andrew, some way behind Tom, heard a yelp as Tom disappeared from sight, the only indication of his presence being the waving tops of the ferns as he tried to free himself from their clutches. His reappearance was spectacular. His head and shoulders shot up above the ferns and his head rotated as he tried to relocate his position in time and space. Andrew was reminded of wildlife programmes he had seen featuring meercats emerging from their burrows, standing erect and looking all around for trouble. Andrew, doubled up with laughter, tried to balance him against a rotting tree trunk as he continued his descent, before himself tumbling into the ferns as the trunk broke. He made a conscious effort not to resemble a meercat as he struggled to his feet.

From the start of the week the chosen hostelry for post-hill, pre-dinner refreshments was the Stronlossit Inn, only a few hundred yards from the chalet at Roy Bridge and well stocked with a range of real ales. By Wednesday it was becoming fairly clear that it would be the venue for the annual dinner, but it seemed necessary to re-check its credentials on a fairly regular basis. The meercats and friends were happy to partake of refreshing drinks on the return home.

The next day was dry and quite sunny, ideal for a return trip to Loch Quoich to climb two Munros. What started as a promising day quickly changed. As the group stretched into single file, spread over a fair distance, Paul experienced a horrible "twang" behind his knee and the problem which had troubled him several years before was back – end of his day on the hill. With Tom sprinting (yes!!) several hundred yards uphill to catch up with Andrew to pass on the news about Paul, he was left in no fit state to continue himself, so he and Paul returned at a leisurely pace to the car, while Andrew went on to meet up with Graham who, by now, had been at the first summit long enough to be concerned about the non-appearance of his colleagues. Of course, there was no mobile phone reception in the area to help communication, just when it was needed most. Andrew and Graham finished the round and met up with the others, commiserating with Paul over refreshments in the Tomdoun Hotel. The owner, who had been there for several years, was able to confirm that a previous lady owner had kept the place in a rather eccentric state, coinciding with memories of earlier visits.

By Friday, Graham had ticked off most of the hills in the area he had hoped to climb that week, leaving only the Monadliath. Visiting Newtonmore to purchase a map, it was decided to tackle the fairly long round of the Glen Banchor summits, rather than the easy Geal Charn in Glen Markie, which might be a possible candidate for Graham's final Munro. Paul's knee was giving him real problems, but he struggled to the first summit, before returning by the same route, leaving the others to wander off into the vast morass of peat forming the broad ridge to the adjoining summits. As usual, it was not long before the group became a procession, Graham in the lead and pulling further ahead by the minute. This became an increasing concern to the others, following on behind, as Graham had the only map in the group.

An occasional break in the cloud and rain permitted some views from the final summit of the day before a descent via the long ridge towards Dalballoch. The path marked on the OS map seemed the sensible descent route, but the "path" was un-defined and it was a long, wet trek down to Glenballoch. As Graham and Tom paused frequently to photograph the variety of flora in the glen, Andrew pressed on to be first back, a unique experience, to meet Paul, who was by now just a little concerned at the late return, particularly with dinner at the Stronlossit Inn waiting.

The return to Roy Bridge was rather later than had been planned and as a result the time available for the beautification process prior to the annual dinner was rather shorter than desired. Nevertheless, the group was reasonably presentable as it arrived at the Stronlossit Inn, later than planned. The meal was notable for its quantity rather than its quality, but very enjoyable nevertheless. Much drink was taken and the annual BSSMC argument was around the issue of the temperature at which wine, red and white, should be served and whether it was reasonable to drink either with ice. While fellow diners could not have failed to hear the argument, they refrained from joining in. They probably observed that there are some with whom it is simply not worth arguing, even over such important topics.

And so another successful week ended. Thirteen more Munros for Graham and some frustration for Paul, with his recurring injury. Andrew was content with his eleven summits and Tom was contemplating his new found position as back marker, almost lapped at times by the Michael Schumaker of the BSSMC – Graham.

Chapter 29

The Old House – Kintail

The usual enquiries had been made over winter 2004/05 to ascertain from Graham which gaps in his Munro list he might like to fill in order to identify a suitable base for the 2005 expedition. Kintail emerged as a surprising option and everyone was content to agree. Eventually, there was agreement that the week of 9th July was mutually acceptable. Even so, Paul would be able to manage only part of the week.

The search for suitable accommodation on the internet threw up "Off the Beaten Track," offering The Old House at Innisachro. From its description it did appear as though it was off the beaten track but it sounded ideal, being located at the head of Loch Duich beyond Morvich.

Saturday 9th July therefore saw the familiar assembly at the Green Welly Stop in Tyndrum, where Andrew met up with the "Glasgow Car" containing Alastair, Tom and Graham. There was general agreement that lunch in the West End Hotel in Fort William would be in order as a visit to the Morrison's supermarket there was required too. Incidentally, over the first twenty seven years or so of the BSSMC, the name of this particular supermarket has changed several times – who would have thought in 1979 that the shelf life of the BSSMC would be longer than that of several supermarket chains! Anyway, lunch was predictable, with Graham ordering scampi, but was more notable for the unsolicited attention of a waiter who seemed to wish to join the conversation round the table. He was not encouraged but nevertheless ended up delivering something of a lecture on the subject of Machiavelli, which BSSMC members greeted with a surprised and atypical silence. Perhaps it was just too early in the week for the annual argument.

The directions which had been provided for The Old House were extremely detailed, the house lying beyond the end of the tarmac road beyond Morvich, across the river and a hundred yards further on sitting below the steep slopes of Beinn Fhada.

It was an interesting house. Downstairs was a comfortable lounge with a piano, a first for the BSSMC (more of which later), some unusual prints and wall hangings and a varied selection of reading material. The kitchen was well equipped and had a good dining table which became the main gathering area. The sleeping accommodation was upstairs but was suitable for only 4, so when Paul arrived later he erected his tent in the small back garden.

Sunday was dreich and the big mountains of Kintail were not attractive in such conditions. Graham had missed out on the ascent of Fionn Bheinn above Achnasheen some years earlier and, as it was recalled as little more than an uphill walk, it was considered a suitable start to the week. It was, of course, some way away from Kintail but that presented coffee shop opportunities. However, no one had brought a map of the Achnasheen area and no one felt inclined to buy one for just that one skittery wee hill. After coffee and home baking in Achnasheen the group set off, encountering a very early obstacle in the shape of a fairly substantial forestry plantation which, from memory, "hadn't been there before." The lack of a map necessitated a bit of guess work to find a route through the trees but it wasn't long before the open shoulder of the hill appeared – in low cloud. Now, what follows is a course of action not recommended to anyone reading this – the group made the ascent using only Tom's GPS, which had not been properly calibrated. It was, though, reassuring to find that the GPS provided more accurate direction than the very general guidance on offer e.g. "if we head south we'll hit the road."

As the usual spread out group arrived back at Achnasheen some 4½ hours later, Alastair and Tom, wearing their colour co-ordinated Rohan clothing, none of which is terribly brightly coloured, were amusingly described by Paul in passing as "The Beige Boys," a description which A and T didn't find flattering but which seemed totally appropriate to the others. As the group consumed afternoon tea, some amused and some miffed at the "Beige Boys" tag, Paul came up with an equally unflattering alternative, based on eating habits. Alastair could be "Bush Tucker Man," from his reputation for self sufficiency while Tom could be "Tea Room Tucker Man," for reasons which should be self-explanatory. Alastair and Tom tried to ignore this nonsense, but the group could not help notice the appearance of brighter and less co-ordinated clothing as the week wore on. Tom added to the merriment by carefully examining the gift shop's selection of amber jewellery, making use of the magnifying glass on his Swiss Army knife, much to the bemusement of the staff, who were not used to this sort of close inspection of their stock by the average tourist.

After dinner back at The Old House the group made its first visit of the week to the bar of the Kintail Lodge Hotel. It hadn't changed much over the years although a welcome addition to the bar was an area set aside for bar meals, which looked promising, as did the menu, for later in the week.

A group of locals, some of whom looked familiar, sat at the bar, looking round each time the door opened to cast an eye over new arrivals. At least one of the locals seemed to have had a drink or two too many. Another engaged in conversation, trying to elicit as much information as he could from the BSSMC members as they ordered at the bar, perhaps hoping for a drink in return for any local advice he could offer. On hearing The Saddle was on the BSSMC agenda for Monday, he advised that the summit would be reached in an hour from Shiel Bridge. Presumably he had never actually made the ascent, at least not on foot.

Monday dawned hot and sunny, rising to 26°C, so it was a hot, sweaty ascent to the Forcan Ridge for an entertaining scramble to the summit of The Saddle. The group descended to the bealach below Sgurr na Sgine, another of Graham's "missing" summits. While Tom walked down the path to return to the cars, the others took in Sgurr Na Sgine, descending by the ridiculously steep, unrelenting and knee punishing shoulder of Faochag, the hill which dominates the view from Glenshiel looking west. The group resisted the temptation to return to the bar at the Kintail Lodge to inform their mountain advisor that their day on the hill had taken 8½ hours. Instead they had an interesting home cooked meal, starring Tom's butternut squash and red pepper stew, which was somewhat enlivened by the addition of rather too much hot red pepper sauce, from a bottle whose warning label had been overlooked by the chef. It just meant more beer had to be consumed.

Tuesday was warm but cloudy. Alastair's knees were complaining from the previous day's efforts and Tom was feeling unfit, so they opted for a day of geological exploration in Glenelg, giving them an excuse to get back into "Beige Boys" uniform without fear of comment from the others. The others had a day on hills to the south of Cluanie. Graham raced off to climb Ciste Dubh on his own, while Andrew and Paul made a more leisurely ascent of Aonach Meadhoin, where Graham re-joined them on the ridge, having timed his route to perfection. An enjoyable day and a further boost to Graham's Munro tally. The Beige Boys fared less well, complaining of having paid £6 each for sandwiches in the Glenelg Inn. One hopes the beer was not equally expensive.

As this was Paul's last day, there was agreement that dinner would be in the bar at the Kintail Lodge Hotel, although the records show that this was not officially the BSSMC annual dinner – that was to come later. The records also show that Graham had haddock and chips despite scampi being on the menu. Sufficient alcohol was consumed for behaviour in the latter stages of the evening to degenerate back at The Old House. The piano's keyboard was exposed and some sheet music was found in the piano stool. No one in the BSSMC can play the piano, but Andrew insisted on trying to play requests made by Alastair and Tom, who, despite being a symphony in beige, were definitely not singing along in the same key. It was a late night!

Paul left early in the morning to return to work. The others opted for a walk to the Falls of Glomach, the path starting right behind the cottage. Graham's route took him over A' Ghlas Beinn, while the elder trio made straight for the falls where he joined them later. A lazy afternoon was spent panning for garnets in the pools above the falls and trying to photograph the inconsiderately high drop of the fall, which doesn't conform to the rectangular configuration of most cameras. Everyone was keen to walk out by a different, perhaps more scenic route, down Glen Elchaig to Killilan, some distance by road from their starting point. With thoughts on which hills which might lie in store for the next day and what the transport implications might be, Andrew indulged in some horse trading - well car trading - with the others, perhaps influenced by the earlier lecture on Machiavelli. Andrew offered to return, alone, to The Old House to collect a car and meet the others later at Killilan. This worked well and everyone enjoyed the day.

At breakfast on Thursday morning Andrew called in his part of the bargain. He and Graham wanted to go to Glen Strathfarrar and would prefer the use of two cars. Tom was not fit for the hill walk involved and Alastair, who was feeling unwell, wanted a day at "home." There was some suspicion that he was hoping the cottage owner might appear for morning coffee and he could pursue his theories about her apparent interest in the occult. Tom agreed to borrow Alastair's car and followed Andrew and Graham on the long drive round to Strathfarrar, where he then drove them further up the glen to allow them a shorter return route to Andrew's car further down the glen. It was a very windy day on the hills with some rain but an enjoyable walk nevertheless.

The final day was dry, cool and grey. Having left one car towards the west end of Loch Cluanie, the group set off together for the summit of Carn Ghlusaid. Once again, Graham raced ahead to take in Tighe Mor na Seilge while the others moved at a more leisurely pace to Sgurr nan Conbhairean, to be re-joined at the summit by Graham. As he arrived it was time for Andrew to depart, getting a head start on Graham for the 1300 ft descent and the climb up to A'Chralaig, where Graham caught him up. The Beige Boys made their descent by the original ascent route and spent the remainder of the day on pseudo-geological ditherings in a quarry near the loch. Meanwhile, Andrew and Graham were leaving their final summit at 15.15 and were in the Cluanie Inn at 16.30 for liquid refreshments.

It was back to the Kintail Lodge Hotel for the official dinner that night, although it was fairly indistinguishable from Tuesday's unofficial dinner. The accounts show an incredibly complicated adjustment to take account of the fact that Alastair and Paul had not shared in any of the wine purchased during the week.

Saturday's journey home allowed time for lunch in the Ben Nevis Bar in Fort William. Over the years its fixed price lunch has offered very good value – straightforward mince for Alastair and fish and chips, to satisfy Graham as a change from scampi. To complete the gluttony, an afternoon stop was made at the Green Welly where the 27th annual expedition of the BSSMC was brought formally to a close.

Chapter 30

The Irish Munros

An expedition to Ireland, to climb all the mountains over 3000 feet, had been discussed for several years. Finally, it was agreed that 2006 would be the year when the trip would be undertaken. Andrew had visited Ireland on a number of occasions and had been in the vicinity of most of the mountains at one time or another, so he had become aware that they were not ideally positioned for a single round. On making enquiries in one outdoor shop about the availability of a suitable guidebook, the idea of climbing all the 3000 footers in one trip was met with some amusement. Apparently, no one in Ireland did that, unless it was part of some charity drive and walk exercise, similar to the "Tree Peaks Race" (or was that just the shop assistant's pronunciation?) in Britain. Instead, walkers and climbers tended to focus on Macgillicuddy's Reeks, the greatest concentration of 3000 foot peaks, or the Connemarra mountains, none of which is over 3000 feet. The BSSMC elected to be different and climb all the "Irish Munros" in a week.

Planning was difficult - nothing new here then! In addition to the usual difficulty of identifying mutually free time, accommodation was a major problem. Having decided to go at the end of May, to avoid school holidays and in the hope of better weather, Andrew discovered that two of the Irish Youth Hostels he had identified didn't open until June. To explain the problem more fully, the mountains fall into four groupings – Lugnaquilla, south of Dublin but in an area which is difficult to access by road from anywhere with identifiable accommodation, The Galty Mountains near Tipperary, Brandon Mountain at the western end of the Dingle peninsula and Macgillicuddy's Reeks near Killarney. As staying in one place wasn't an option and moving on from place to place left the potential problem of lost days due to bad weather, which seemed inevitable in Ireland, a ten day trip was agreed to allow for a two centre trip, travel between bases and bad weather days.

Andrew identified a privately run hostel called Otterholt Riverside Lodge in Carlow as a compromise location for access to Lugnaquilla and The Galtees, albeit involving long drives to both, for the first three nights. From there a long drive to a rented house near Killorglin would follow, with Killorglin being a good base for access to Macgillicuddy's Reeks and reasonably close to the Dingle peninsula.

Otterholt Riverside Lodge was booked for three nights for a group of five, although at the time of booking it remained a bit unclear who the five would be. There was a slight concern about the standard of accommodation as several comments on the booking website suggested it was a bit run down, but that was unlikely to trouble the roughty-toughties of the BSSMC. The house at Cromane Upper, near Killorglin, was called White Sands and at only £288 for the week it seemed rather too cheap for the spacious accommodation apparently on offer, so perhaps there would be some nasty surprise waiting there.

After months of planning, Tom, whose flight from Cardiff had been changed at the last minute, adding to his growing distrust of low cost airlines, was first to arrive at Dublin Airport, to be joined by Roderick, who had flown from Manchester. They collected a rental car and drove to Carlow. Meanwhile, Andrew, Graham and Paul met at Edinburgh Airport for an uneventful flight, other than Graham's surprise announcement during the flight that he was about to become a dad. A second rental car was collected at Dublin and this second group set off for Carlow. Phone contact with Tom, who had by now arrived at the Lodge, led the second group to think that concerns over the standard of accommodation may well have been justified. Arrival confirmed their worst fears. The grounds, of what must once have been a fine building, were overgrown and the parking areas were occupied by a fleet of vintage Rolls Royces adorned with bridal ribbons and floral arrangements. The entrance area was shabby, not to say dirty. The poorly equipped kitchen was filthy, barely furnished and featured a tiny television, around which sat a group of Eastern Europeans watching a foreign language channel while eating from tins which were being opened with a large bread knife. The adjacent office housed a cheerful Englishman who seemed to be in charge of the place. He took the money and promised that any necessary cooking and eating utensils would be supplied on request – they weren't left out as they tended to disappear. Fortunately the dormitory, with a mixture of bunk beds and small single beds, was reasonably clean, although some of the bunks were held together with strategically positioned pieces of 4 x 2. The toilets and showers had probably been state of the art in the 1960s but appeared not to have had much done to them, including cleaning, since.

The decision to eat out that evening was a fairly easy one and some shopping in the local supermarket was restricted to packed lunch materials and ingredients for a cold buffet breakfast, which could be eaten involving minimal contact with any surfaces inside Otterholt Riverside Lodge. After a few pints and a good bar meal, the BSSMC assembled in a large second kitchen back at the Lodge for a few drams and a discussion about plans for the next few days. This kitchen had been identified as a possible venue for meals, as it was marginally less dirty than the other one, but the facilities were, at best, basic and there were still no cooking utensils, so the decision to continue to eat out while in Carlow was easily made. Fortunately the weather forecast for the next few days was good.

As BSSMC members awoke next morning, to a beautiful, warm and sunny day, the eastern Europeans, who seemed to be migrant workers, were preparing sandwiches prior to leaving by minibus for work, presumably in local agriculture. Selecting carefully from the few available plates, mugs and cutlery, a buffet breakfast was taken and a hasty departure made in the direction of Lugnaquilla.

The drive was fairly tortuous, though very scenic and it seemed to take for ever to reach Glen Malur, the preferred starting point for the ascent. Lugnaquilla is slap, bang in the middle of an artillery firing range and the BSSMC had taken some account of this in planning a route. It was, therefore, with some annoyance and frustration that at the entrance to the glen a huge red flag was flying above a notice board announcing that when the red flag was flying, any person found entering the area would, at very least, be charged with serious sounding offences, incarcerated and possibly even shot at dawn. Several attempts were made to contact the Range Warden on the advertised phone number but mobile phone reception was, to say the least, patchy in the glen and when contact was eventually made the message of the red flag was re-enforced. The weather was perfect and to abandon the day would not only be a waste but would throw the mountaineering schedule into chaos – this was the one day which could not easily be re-arranged.

After an abortive attempt to meet the Range Warden to plead a case for limited access, it was observed that a few vehicles had come down the glen and that as a hostel was shown on the map it was assumed that it would be safe to proceed at least as far as the hostel to make further enquiries. On the drive up the glen the two cars were accompanied by low flying helicopters at several points, adding to the feeling of apprehension that arrest, or worse, was imminent. Nevertheless, progress was made to the end of the road and the group advanced tentatively towards the hostel, which was closed. Nearby, however, was a group (or should that be a convoy?) of military vehicles, including several ambulances, with only one soldier visible. Even then, it was difficult to identify him positively as a soldier; he was stripped to the waist, exposing his excessively flabby torso to the sun, apparently asleep on a stretcher which had been removed from a nearby army ambulance. A colleague was sitting inside the ambulance, reading a newspaper. The sleeping soldier opened one eye at the sound of the advancing ranks of the BSSMC and raised himself on one elbow in response to a tentative enquiry about possible access to Lugnaquilla.

Initially he said that access would not be possible as "heavy artillery fire" was taking place, involving firing into the hillside. While this was happening "snipers" would be coming in from all angles to try to take out the gun crews without being seen by the "spotters" who were strategically placed all over the mountain. The presence of the BSSMC would not be welcome in such circumstances, apparently, and might even be dangerous.

After further discussion and close scrutiny of a map, a possible safe route of ascent and return was identified, more or less the route that had been planned in the first place. The ambulance crew had to obtain permission from "the Sarge", who came over and eyed the foreign forces suspiciously. Finally he gave reluctant permission with a stern warning that to depart from the agreed route would quite likely have fatal consequences, or at least a very long jail sentence.

It was early afternoon before a start was made, ascending through a forest and over moorland to a pretty loch for a very late lunch. From there it was a fairly easy moorland walk to the summit. Periodically the thump of heavy artillery fire impacting the opposite side of the hill could be heard and near the summit there was a distinct smell of whatever gunfire smells like. The slope to the summit was also littered with shallow depressions which were clearly craters caused by artillery fire which had overshot the ridge. This did not inspire confidence.

Nearing the summit of the BSSMC's first Irish "Munro", it was with some apprehension that four men were spotted heading for the summit from the opposite direction – the direction of the firing range. Could they be snipers arriving to take out the invading BSSMC forces or Military Police to make arrests? No, they were four elderly gentlemen, smelling strongly of alcohol, who walked up from the edge of the firing range regularly on a Thursday, when they were unable to play golf as it was ladies' day at the golf club. They didn't bother seeking permission and just ignored red flags as they were quite adamant that the firing range was nowhere near where they would be walking.

The remainder of the day was something of an anti climax, the long drive back to Carlow via a pub being followed by a quick clean up at the hovel – sorry, hostel – before another evening out in Carlow.

Another sunny day on Friday signalled an early departure for the long drive to The Galty Mountains with a brief stop for provisions in Kilkenny. Alastair had been in contact to say he was in Dublin where he had spent the night and arrangements were made to meet him in Kilkenny on the return journey later that day. He would travel down by train, but couldn't understand why he could not simply get off the train in Carlow. He was informed that it would be in his best interests to spend time waiting for the others in Kilkenny rather than in the delightful Otterholt Riverside Lodge, although having just returned from Kazakhstan he may well have felt at home there.

Access to the Galty Mountains was via a "bohreen" or narrow farm lane on the north side of the range. To avoid any doubt, a farmer driving a very large, expensive looking tractor, was asked if the bohreen was the correct one (there were several in the vicinity) by which to access the mountain. He wasn't sure, but recalled having seen walkers head up there previously and assumed they must have been going up the hill, although he could not understand why anyone would want to go to the summit just for fun. He was encountered at several points on the road up exchanging cheery conversation and driving on ahead each time with a wave. Even after just two days in the area the BSSMC had observed that all the agricultural machinery they had seen seemed to be state of the art and had that very expensive look about it. The people operating the machinery or encountered on farmland all looked, however, as though they did not have two euro to rub together.

The hot, sunny weather made the colours of the flowering gorse and hawthorn even more vibrant and there were frequent stops for fine views and photographs on the otherwise tedious plod to the summit ridge where the view in all directions was magnificent. A circular route enabled a pleasant ridge walk and a descent via another bohreen back to the cars. The journey and day on the hill had taken rather longer than anticipated, so Alastair had had a long wait and a few pints before the main group joined him in Kilkenny for an excellent meal in a huge bar/café/entertainment venue in the Langton House Hotel which had been recommended by Graham, who was familiar with Kilkenny. Eventually, a return to Otterholt Riverside Lodge had to be made. Alastair's arrival had been announced to the "warden" earlier but, as he wasn't seen again before leaving next morning, it was felt unnecessary to pursue him to pay for Alastair's bed night. It was, therefore, with some relief that the BSSMC left Carlow on the Saturday morning for the long drive to Killorglin, stopping at Cashel en route for photos of the magnificent ruined monastery.

After the disastrous accommodation in Carlow, it was with a certain amount of trepidation the group drove through Killorglin and on to Cromane Upper. The house bearing the name White Sands was a modern house set in a large garden. It looked rather too big and comfortable to be home to the BSSMC for only £288, but a knock at the door of a large, nearby bungalow roused Mrs. Foley, who confirmed that this was indeed the house. She gave a conducted tour. A long, L-shaped hall with a dining room and double doors led through to a very large, well equipped kitchen and utility room. Along the hall were a bedroom and a bathroom. Upstairs were three further bedrooms, each with an en suite shower room, and a comfortably furnished lounge with doors opening on to a small balcony above the large garden with a truly magnificent view across the adjacent meadow, the lough beyond and on to Macgillicuddy's Reeks in the distance. This was, without doubt, the most spacious, comfortable and well equipped accommodation ever occupied by the BSSMC and in a magnificent location.

A quick return trip to Killorglin, situated on the River Laune, revealed a fairly limited choice of grocery shops, but adequate for the needs of the BSSMC. For a small town, the sports facilities in and around the town seemed excellent. Of particular note was the Gaelic Athletic Association ground, home of the local Gaelic football team who rejoiced in the name of "The Laune Rangers."

The good weather was still holding, so it was decided to tackle one half of Macgillicuddy's Reeks, a traverse of the whole range in one day presenting not only transport difficulties but being beyond the fitness levels of the older members of the group. The day's route involved a traverse of the eastern horseshoe, comprising Beenkeragh, the airy scramble along to Carrauntoohill and a long descent via Caher. Beautiful views, fine ridges, excellent summits and warm, sunny weather made for a most enjoyable day.

After dinner at White Sands the only entertainment on offer lay at the local pub, where Andrew, Paul, Graham and Rod arrived at around 9.30pm, remarking on how quiet it was. The barman said it was "still early." He was correct. Locals arrived later, providing music on fiddles, accordions and guitar for a lively end to the evening. On returning to White Sands, Alastair, who had stayed behind with Tom, was keen to know if the others had found any "craik" at the pub. He had heard that "craik" was prevalent in Ireland, although he wasn't terribly sure what it was. He was assured that "craik" would be waiting for him at the pub should he choose to sample it.

It was almost beyond belief that Monday dawned warm and sunny too, so it was agreed that the opportunity should be taken to climb Brandon Mountain, a hill more frequently exposed to wind and rain from the Atlantic. It was a fairly long but very scenic drive out through Dingle and over the Connor pass to Cloghane, where the starting point for the route was located with the help of Graham's GPS, guidebooks, maps and much discussion. The so called "Pilgrims' Route" started off on a good path which led into an extremely impressive, rocky corrie, up the back wall of the corrie on a mixture of short scrambles and loose scree, which Rod did not enjoy, to a coll just a hundred feet below the summit. The views of the beaches and coastline, with the Skellig Islands beyond, were truly magnificent, the blue of the sea almost unbelievable.

The group split at the summit. Paul and Alastair returned by the same route to retrieve the cars, Tom and Andrew continued over Brandon Peak with Graham, who then left them to follow the remaining tops on the ridge leading to the Connor Pass, while the two elders descended to the Cloghane Valley, to be collected by Paul and Alastair, who had driven round. Roderick descended by the "Saint's Road" to the south, with a promise that he would be collected later. Arrangements had also been made to meet Graham at the Connor Pass car park on completion of his longer walk. The purpose of describing the various descent routes is to illustrate how complicated the logistics can become on what should be a straightforward day out. Anyway, all agreed it had been a memorable day, which was topped off with a good meal in Murphy's Bar (imaginative name) in Dingle, as it was adjudged to be too late to be returning to White Sands to eat.

With four full days remaining and only one day required to climb the remaining summits on Macgillicuddy's Reeks, a day off was considered in order, the only reservation being that the weather was perfect again. While Alastair elected to stay at White Sands, the others set off for a circular tour taking in Killarney, Moll's Gap, the Gap of Dunloe, jaunting cars, American tourists, cakes, scones and so on. Later in the evening the whole group visited the local pub, where Alastair held open the door to allow the very old and extremely smelly resident dog to join the BSSMC table inside, to the obvious disgust of the other drinkers. Alastair remained unsure whether there had been any "craik" that night. It certainly hadn't been apparent during Alastair's chat with the dog.

Unbelievably, Wednesday was another day of perfect weather and Macgilicuddy's Reeks beckoned across the lough. The starting point for the day was a small farm at the top of a bohreen, where the elderly lady occupant had a nice earner selling cold drinks, chocolate bars, postcards and charging a couple of euro for parking cars in the yard. Meanwhile the men on the farm were using state of the art tools and equipment to renovate an outbuilding, presumably with some tourist-related activity in mind.

A path and a straightforward ascent across some moorland led to the lip of Lough Cummeennapeasta, from where the route for the rest of the day could be seen. The ridge above looked interesting, too interesting for Rod, who elected for a low level day, arranging to meet the others later in the afternoon. After about 1500 feet or so of very steep ascent the "summit group" reached the first top of the day, Cruach Mhor, with its hand built stone grotto standing some 15 feet tall and visible from everywhere on the ridge. Then came the trickiest part of the ridge, several airy scrambles to a top called "Big Gun" before reaching the summits of Lackagarrin and Cummeennapeasta, the final "Irish Munro." There is a great deal of confusion over the naming of the tops which make up Macgillycuddy's Reeks, with different books and maps adopting variations on names and sometimes using different names altogether, but the traverse of two final tops ensured that all the recognised 3000 foot tops had been climbed.

The group descended to Lough Callee where they rejoined Roderick for the walk back to the cars via a path leading down Hag's glen. It had been a most enjoyable day on a ridge equal to some of the best in Scotland and it ensured the objective of climbing all the "Irish Munros" had been achieved with several days to spare, leaving time for some tourist activity.

Thursday 8th June was another beautiful, sunny day so two carloads of tourists set off from White Sands for a very scenic trip along the south shore of Dingle Bay to Valentia Island via a short crossing on the car ferry. Valentia was very interesting as well as being very pretty. Points of interest included the location of the first transatlantic cable station in 1858 and the world famous fossil trackway, fossilised footprints of tetrapods – primitive four legged vertebrates thought to be the first to leave aquatic environments and breathe air on land. The trackway is at least 385 million years old but was discovered only as recently as 1993. Of even greater interest to several members of the group was the excellent pub lunch in the Knightstown Coffee Shop nearby and the Portmagee Village Public Facility which was runner up in Ireland's 2002 Top Toilet Award.

Thursday was rounded off with an excellent BSSMC annual dinner in the Bianconi Inn in Killorglin, at a total cost of 279 Euro and 30 cents, including tip. The perfect week concluded with the mother and father of all thunderstorms shortly after the group returned to White Sands late that evening. Huge forks of lightning illuminated Macgillycuddy's Reeks accompanied by deafening thunder – it was quite a finale to the week, with one further day to spare.

On Friday, everyone apart from Graham was happy to enjoy another fester. Graham had made some enquiries about hiring a bike for the day, so the others dropped him at the bike rental shop in Killarney before they went on to the grounds of the picturesque Muckross Castle. Meanwhile Graham went on a strenuous Tour de Kerry followed by a run back to White Sands – an exhausting day but memorable for him.

All that remained was to clear up on the Saturday, with Mrs. Foley complementing the group on how tidy they had left the house and how they had recycled waste in accordance with instructions. To be honest, it would have been embarrassing to have left behind the mountain of empty beer cans, so they had been disposed of discreetly, out of Mrs. Foley's sight. The drive back to Dublin was fairly tedious with a stop for lunch in Nenagh before everyone went their various ways at Dublin Airport, some having chosen to stay on in Ireland for a while longer – but that's another story.

Chapter 31

A Wet Week in Blair Atholl

The 2007 annual expedition will not go down in BSSMC history as one of the best. There was very little to make it memorable. First of all there was considerable doubt about who would be there – no Alastair, Graham uncertain because of work commitments, Tom and Paul doubtful for similar reasons. At one point it was beginning to look as though Andrew might be taking Audrey for an unplanned holiday in Blair Atholl, where a cottage had been booked as late as May when it had seemed a turnout of three or four might be possible.

As 12th July approached the final roll call was Andrew and Tom with Paul arriving for the second half of the week. Tom flew to Edinburgh where Andrew met him and the pair drove to Pitlochry to collect a key for Orchard Cottage in Blair Atholl. A bedroom each was a luxury and the kitchen was extremely well equipped, so comfort was guaranteed and there was ample opportunity to put culinary skills to the test. Andrew and Tom rose to the challenge and the resulting meals were of a high standard – or did they just drink more wine than usual?

The best and only dry day was Sunday. With no great levels of fitness a fairly easy day seemed in order so it was agreed they would fulfil a long standing ambition to climb Ben Vrackie. Starting from the car park above Moulin, the walk to the summit was easy, even allowing for a detour to the north for views of Killiecrankie. The stone staircase from the loch to the summit came as something of a surprise but what must it be like when wet or in winter? The views from the top were magnificent, with the Pentlands being visible to the south and Ben Nevis to the north west. The pair lingered for a while on the various tops enjoying the panoramas before descending, choosing to avoid the stone staircase in the interests of knee preservation. A refreshment in the Moulin Inn and an excellent evening meal finished off an extremely enjoyable day. It was to be all downhill from then.

The next day was very wet and a walk to the falls of Bruar was interesting if hardly enjoyable in the rain, although perhaps the best sort of weather in which to see the falls at their most spectacular, in spate. Wednesday's forecast was similar, so another low level walk, this time to see the waterfall at the Hermitage, was the day's chosen activity. As luck would have it, the weather improved as the day wore on and allowed an extended walk, first to the falls at Rumbling Bridge then a visit to Neil Gow's tree next to the River Tay, with its interestingly inscribed bench, followed by a walk through the ancient oak forest into Dunkeld, where it was warm enough to eat outside by the river. Paul arrived at Orchard Cottage that evening in time for another excellent meal.

Paul hadn't been up Schiehallion and it had been a longstanding wish of Andrew's to actually see the view from the summit. On his three or four previous visits low cloud or rain had obscured the view. The forecast suggested rain later in the day but Schiehallion wasn't a long day, so off they went, parking at the Braes of Foss. During the walk up, Andrew and Tom reminisced over one ascent in the early 1970s when Andrew had cut his finger quite badly while opening a sardine tin. Sardines were a staple in those days and Andrew had a habit of cutting his fingers while opening the tin. It was quite remarkable then when Paul found the rusting remains of a sardine tin amongst the summit boulders – would there be traces of Andrew's DNA on it? And would they simply have discarded the offending tin at the summit? Sadly, with green credentials not having been invented in the '70s, it was quite usual for rubbish to be "buried" under stones, often at the summit, so this could be the actual tin. And there was a view from the summit, for at least a few minutes, but for a fairly limited distance. The rain became progressively heavier on the return to the car, but another fine meal back at Orchard Cottage helped raise spirits (and copious amounts of spirits helped raise the meal too).

More rain on Thursday encouraged lethargy. Coffee in the rather forlorn hotel in Dalwhinnie was followed by an afternoon dash up Geal Charn, further enhancing the reputation of hills bearing that name for being wet and forgettable. The return journey through Pitlochry presented the opportunity for the BSSMC putting competition to take place on the infamous hilly course. The course was made even more challenging by being waterlogged, so scores were not good – perhaps something of an understatement.

Beinn a' Ghlo was so close at hand that it would have been a shame to miss the opportunity to climb it but the weather was, yet again, overcast at best. Tom needed a lot of persuasion but eventually the group left for an 8 hour trip round all the tops. At several points Tom had to be persuaded to continue. He kept coming up with alternative routes, all of which involved descent, but with much bullying from the others he carried on. The route back to the car was something of a wet slog, but the prospect of the annual BSSMC dinner provided some incentive to keep moving.

The dinner was in the Atholl Arms Hotel, pretty much Hobson's choice, but at least within walking distance. The bar was cosy and had a nice enough atmosphere, but the long wait to be served gave ample time to observe a single filthy dishcloth being used repeatedly, without cleaning, to wipe round the edge of beer glasses after it had been used to clean the counter. When the issue of hygiene was raised with the Eastern European bar staff their grasp of English deteriorated and it seemed that no one was in overall charge, so the observation/complaint fell on deaf ears. The dining room was soul-less and, although the food was reasonable it did not arrive without incident. One of the starter courses arrived without the promised oatcakes, the wine was not the one which had been ordered and the waiting staff had to be reminded several times that main courses had not been served (it emerged that they had been forgotten somewhere along the line). The standard of service was pretty awful so it was hardly surprising that Tom had a bit of a rant - to no one in particular.

With comfortable accommodation and excellent home cooked meals, the week had not been as bad as the weather had tried to make it. And Ben Vrackie deserves to be a Munro, despite it being only 640 metres high.

Brandon Mountain, Dingle Peninsula, Ireland

Macgillycuddy's Reeks (west) from Cnoc an Chuilinn

Macgillycuddy's Reeks from Cromane Upper

Tom at lochan on Ben Vrackie

Andrew's hat burns on Skiddaw

Graham's Compleation on Ruadh Stac Mhor

Alastair Macrae

Tom Sharpe

Graham Freeland

Andrew Vickery

Paul Forrest

Roderick MacKenzie

Just Guess!

Has anyone seen the BSSMC?

Chapter 32

Onich Yet Again

2008 would be the year of the 30th annual expedition of the BSSMC – not the thirtieth anniversary, that would be in 2009 (please feel free to put this book down to free up all your fingers to work out the arithmetic). There had been a brief notion of trying to arrange something on the grand scale, but this was soon dismissed as impractical. Indeed, attendance became so uncertain that at one point only Alastair and Andrew were sure of turning up at Croft Cottage in Onich during the week of 12th July. As the date approached, Graham and Tom confirmed their attendance.

Travel arrangements were relatively straightforward for a change. Alastair would collect Tom from Glasgow Airport and Andrew would pick up Graham then meet at the cottage around 4pm. Some shopping had been done in advance and both cars were full for the short trip north. Although not pre-arranged, the two groups met up at the Green Welly Stop and travelled together over Rannoch Moor and through Glencoe.

The weather forecast for the week did not look good, with Saturday 12th appearing to be the best day, so there was no great optimism about the week. No one could have foreseen the first low point of the week however. Just west of Ballachuillish traffic came to a halt and drivers coming in the opposite direction were indicating that the road was closed due to an accident. Telephone calls to various contacts, including the caretaker at Croft Cottage, suggested the road would be closed for several hours although it was unclear where the accident had occurred. Andrew and Graham elected to sit in the virtually stationary queue while Alastair and Tom opted for a scenic detour via Kinlochleven – and ended up stationary on the other side of the loch. The accident (with at least one fatality) had been between the bridge and Onich and a helicopter had been used to evacuate casualties. Eventually traffic began to flow and Alastair and Tom justified their long diversion by arriving about twenty minutes before the others.

The cottage had three bedrooms. The two attic rooms were accessed by the steepest, narrowest and most awkward stair ever encountered by the BSSMC. Wisely, Alastair had quickly claimed the downstairs room, leaving the other three to negotiate the V. Diff ascent and descent of the staircase for the rest of the week (as it turned out, only Andrew managed to fall down it). Otherwise, the cottage was ideal, with an excellent dining kitchen and adequate drying space – which would be well used.

Graham's list of "to do" Munros seemed to be growing annually rather than reducing. as he had not recorded ascents during his early years on the hills, but his memory seemed to be worryingly vague for one so young. He was also reaching the stage where he was making doubly sure where he had doubts. Surprisingly, it seemed that he hadn't been up all the tops in the Blackmount.

The weather on Sunday was dry and bright, so a Blackmount trip seemed like a good idea. By coincidence, Alastair and Andrew had both harboured a desire to climb straight up the front of Sron na Creise. Surprisingly, this route had never featured in Alastair's catalogue of direct ascents. So this was the chosen route for the day, at least for Alastair, Andrew and Graham. Tom was feeling particularly unfit and was incubating what turned out to be the most horrible, cough-ridden, flu-type thing one could imagine, so he opted for a chairlift ride and a short walk to the summit of Meall a Bhuirde, from where he watched the progress of the others through binoculars.

The day began with a river crossing, several miles into Glen Etive. Graham found a route and bounced across safely, preparing his camera for photos of Andrew immersing one foot into the river and Alastair undertaking a painful wade having opted to remove his boots. Pausing only to allow Andrew to change into dry socks, the route was pretty much straight up, with a few scrambles near the top. Visibility was good and Tom could be seen over on Meall a Bhuirde watching progress. Graham continued over Creise to Clach Leathad, another of his "not sure" summits before the whole group re-assembled on Meall a'Bhuirde. The descent to the car park was made more interesting due to a downhill mountain bike event taking place. If there are going to be huge ruts and channels due to overuse it seems quite reasonable that they should be made worse by allowing, indeed supporting, several hundred suicidal (mainly male) loonies to hurtle downhill on machines which vaguely resemble bicycles. It was, however, fairly entertaining to watch.

That was the end of any decent weather for the week. Monday was overcast and the forecast promised rain in the west. Heading east seemed the best option, although Alastair elected to stay at home. The others drove to the Spey Dam near Laggan from where an ascent of Geall Charn was the plan. This hill, no more than a walk, had been kept as a possible final Munro for Graham, being a short, easy day but plans for that event would now have to change. Tom's flu was beginning to develop so he had a gentle walk up Glen Markie from the Spey Dam while Graham and Andrew took in the hill in four and a half hours – cloudy, cold, damp but not really any rain. The long drive back gave plenty opportunity for Tom to spread his germs in the confined space of the car.

It rained for the rest of the week and Tom coughed for the rest of the week, struggling on as best he could. On Wednesday Graham and Andrew had a walk to see the waterfall at Steall in full flow, intending to meet Alastair who had left earlier with a similar plan. En route, they upheld the tradition of lunch in the West End Hotel in Fort William, where the menu has changed little in twenty years. However, Graham was pleased to see that it now included vegetable samosas. By the time phone contact was made, Alastair was on the summit of Ben Nevis having, in his usual way, changed his plan.

Graham didn't want another idle day so, although Thursday was another dreich day, he decided to go for a run – up Bidean nan Bian. He left from the car park at the entrance to the Lost Valley, dressed in his fell running shoes, compression running trousers and light poloneck, carrying little more than water. The occupants of parked cars watched in amazement as he ran up the path on Aonach Dubh, passing several groups of walkers who had left the car park at least an hour earlier. The crowd continued to watch until Graham disappeared into the mist – which wasn't long. Andrew and Tom spent some time at the National Trust centre in Glencoe then waited at the Clachaig Inn for Graham's return, which seemed no time at all.

The rain continued on Friday. Alastair and Tom, donning their "Beige Boys" uniforms, went on a geological expedition to Ardnamurchan while Andrew and Graham checked out local venues for the annual dinner, finally settling for the Loch Leven Hotel. The fixed price dinner at £20 a head was good value. Fellow diners would, no doubt, be wondering in a week or so where they picked up such a horrible cough. Andrew and Alastair experienced it for the remains of the summer, or what was supposed to be summer.

Glen Etive from Creise

Chapter 33

The Thirtieth Anniversary – The Lake District

With the first BSSMC Annual Expedition having been in 1979, 2009 would be the thirtieth anniversary of the "Club." Thoughts of trying to organise a grand gathering of members and friends were quickly dismissed and with work commitments ruling out Paul and Alastair, it was left to founder members Andrew, Roderick and Tom, along with Graham, to form the 2009 group. There remained the possibility of Gavin Steven and Bill Brown joining in for a day or so. The BSSMC had never been about large numbers or large groups, so a gathering of five or six was perfectly acceptable.

Since completing the Irish 3000 ft tops in 2006, only a couple of hills in the Lake District stood in the way of Andrew and Tom completing all the "3000 ft tops furth of Scotland", so the Lake District was a tempting venue for the 2009 expedition. Luckily a cottage was identified offering, fairly unusually, Friday to Friday accommodation, an arrangement which suited everyone and allowed Gavin and Bill to participate, albeit briefly. The cottage, Mell Fell View, was located in the small hamlet of Troutbeck, midway between Penrith and Keswick (there are several Troutbecks in the Lake District, but this particular Troutbeck offers access to most of the area, apart from Wasdale).

On Friday 12th June the troops began to assemble. From the north came Graham and Andrew, while Tom travelled from Wales. Roderick would arrive from Manchester the following day while Gavin would be coming from Wetherby.

Mell Fell View was a very well appointed and spacious former farm cottage with three bedrooms, one with en-suite facilities, allowing unrestricted snoring opportunities for everyone, at least for the first night. The others kindly agreed Graham could occupy the master suite alone to offer him the chance of some quiet, uninterrupted sleep – with his son Jack being 2 years old he welcomed the opportunity. The well equipped kitchen presented a first for the BSSMC, an AGA stove. While it seemed fairly challenging at first, it provided constant hot water, heat (too much at times) and an efficient method of cooking. Those unfamiliar with AGA ovens should, however, be aware of the ease with which one can burn one's arms on the edges while moving food in and out of the ovens.

On the Saturday, Andrew, Graham and Tom set off for the rather long drive round to Wasdale, to climb Scafell and Scafell Pike. It was very overcast, damp and thundery – far from ideal. A torrential downpour between Cockermouth and Cleater Moor did not auger well for the day ahead, but despite Tom's frequent requests for a coffee stop, the trio pressed on to Wasdale Head for a 10.50 start up Scafell Pike, with anything above 2000 ft blanketed in thick mist and low cloud. The BSSMC members were quite unused to the huge numbers of people climbing the hill. The noise of chatter and clattering of walking poles on rock destroyed any feeling of peace while litter, banana skins predominantly, lay all around. To be fair, however, there was little non-degradable rubbish eg polythene or sweet wrappers. A surprising number of dogs were making the ascent – Westies, Border Terriers, Alsations, Labradors, Spaniels, Jack Russells, Collies and everything in between.

The path to the summit was tedious and the summit itself was congested. It was impossible to count exact numbers but there were well over 100 people at the top, close to the 165 present on Andrew's previous visit some 36 years earlier over an Easter weekend with Derek Osborne. Damp cloud, lack of visibility and time constraints encouraged a speedy departure for the narrow coll, Mickledore, the point from which Andrew had previously gained access to Scafell. Unfortunately his memory had failed to record the potential difficulty of the climb from Mickledore to the summit via Broad Stand, a tricky, exposed slab. Having finally located it, there was little doubt that it was not an option, particularly with the rock being very wet. The alternative tourist route, Lord's Rake, proved to be a damp, dirty and tiresome rising traverse below the cliffs of Scafell.

At the summit one of the many stone shelters served as a lunch stop but as conditions remained damp and cloudy there was no good reason to linger long on the litter strewn summit, After an initial descent through the cloud, each of the three amigos chose a slightly different route to the car at Wasdale Head. Needless to say, Graham was first back, in greatly improved weather conditions.

Rather later than anticipated the trio met up with Roderick and Gavin back at the Troutbeck Inn, the two having arrived earlier. The meal in the Inn was very good, although in response to Gavin's request for a "very rare" steak ie "blue" with no mushrooms, he was served a medium steak with mushrooms. He didn't eat the mushrooms, but seemed happy enough with his steak.

It was apparent over dinner that Gavin was deeply infatuated by his "Blackberry" but although he was well and truly immersed in 21st century living he was less than impressed that the BSSMC didn't sleep in sleeping bags or eat dried food any more – he was even taken aback next morning to see the table being set properly for breakfast.

Fortunately Sunday 14th June was a dry sunny day. This was the day which had been set aside for Andrew and Tom to complete the "Furths" with an ascent of Skiddaw, from the congested and rather inadequate car park above Lattrig. It soon became apparent why Skiddaw had never really been considered as a "must do" by the Munro Baggers in the group. The path up was of motorway standard, with motorway volumes of traffic. It seemed particularly popular with fell runners who skilfully navigated lane changes through slow moving and oncoming traffic. It didn't take long to reach the summit, where it was still dry and sunny but quite cold and windy.

For as long as can be remembered, Andrew had worn an increasingly tatty and very faded pink sun hat on the hills. It had often been mocked and derided by the others and on at least one occasion had been threatened with death by incineration. Some years earlier, Andrew had promised he would burn it himself on "compleation" of all the 3000 ft mountains in Britain and Ireland. This promise seemed to have been forgotten by the others but Andrew had remembered and had come equipped with matches and a firelighter to facilitate the cremation. Finding a sheltered spot in one of the stone shelters near the summit, Andrew set the funeral pyre. The firelighter was superfluous as the tattered remains of the hat, which by now was almost in two pieces – the crown almost detached from the rim – seemed content to burn by itself, fuelled by decades of sun cream and midge repellent solvents. Sparks flew as years of accumulated sweat and dirt were consumed by the flames. The firelighter merely added to the pall of black, acrid smoke as the hat burned to ashes. It was hardly surprising that the ceremony began to attract interest from other walkers at the summit. The explanation that an old friend was being cremated drew shocked looks, with visions of pet dogs or perhaps even departed climbing companions flashing through twisted minds. Those sufficiently interested pressed for further details.

The day still being young there was time for a snooze on a sheltered spot on the descent – a sure sign of advancing years. Each descended at his own pace down the still busy motorway and the day was over by 2pm. Even allowing for ceremonial burning and snooze time, the ascent of Skiddaw had taken only 4 hours and 10 minutes, leaving time for a refreshing pint on the way home.

The annual BSSMC dinner was held that night in the Horse and Farrier at Threlkeld, with Bill and Jean Brown joining the group as honoured guests (they had been assessing a Duke of Edinburgh Award expedition around the Keswick area). A very enjoyable meal, the most expensive item being the wine at £19.50 per bottle. The group was very grateful to Gavin who drove – he was returning home late that night, probably disgusted at the levels of comfort and good food in which the BSSMC indulged these days. After Gavin's departure the question was posed – had he really been feeding his Blackberry titbits of food under the table during dinner at the Horse and Farrier?

Next day was mainly dry and sunny in the Keswick area although heavy showers could be seen all round about. For once the BSSMC was in the right place at the right time, so a circuit of the Grisedale hills was planned. While Andrew and Graham opted for a start over the grand viewpoint of Barrow followed by Sail and Crag Hill, Tom and Rod walked up the valley to look at the old mines before meeting the others on Sand Hill. Meantime Graham had gone off to take in Grasmoor. The whole group returned to Braithwaite more or less together for a refreshment in a nice looking pub where the exchange rate against the Scottish pound was extremely unfavourable, or perhaps they just liked to rip off tourists. Shandy cost the same as beer and the price of lemonade on its own made one think a crate from a local supermarket would have been a much cheaper option. The AGA was put to use in the evening for an excellent meal, let down only by the wine, which was corked (it was later returned to the supermarket in Penrith and exchanged).

The objective now was to ensure Graham completed the English 3000ft peaks, so Helvellyn was Tuesday's chosen hill. The biggest problem of the day was undoubtedly finding somewhere to park in Patterdale, but by 10am the group was on the move for the ascent via Striding Edge. As the Edge drew into view it became apparent that a booking system will be required before too long as the queues are becoming quite silly – one could easily get an accidental kick in the face from the boot of the person in front and if a foot was left stationary for too long it was likely to be used as a handhold by someone. Rod didn't fancy the look of the final rocky stretch – had it been quieter it would have been fine – so he turned back for a gentle stroll back to Patterdale. Deciding to pass some time and quench his thirst at the same time, he went into the Patterdale Hotel for a drink, forgetting he had left his money in the locked car. Being aware of the extortionate price of drinks he asked the barman how much lemonade he might get for 80 pence – half a pint, he was told. Sensibly, Rod chatted to the barman and spun him the tale about friends joining him later, when he would be able to pay for his next drink, a story the barman had heard before more than a few times. Having an honest face, Rod was believed and he managed to have another drink on credit.

Meanwhile, the other three were lunching with the assembled masses on the summit of Helvellyn. Having plenty time, they decided to descend via Dollywaggon, simply because it had such a good name. At Grisedale Tarn Graham decided to make his day worthwhile by taking in four or five more tops while Andrew and Tom had a pleasant walk down the lovely Grisedale valley. They reached the Patterdale Hotel just about in time to validate Rod's credit worthiness.

Wednesday was, as forecast, wet so a rest day was agreed. After a brief visit to the supermarket in Penrith for some supplies and to return the corked wine, the group drove to The Old Crown at Hesket Newmarket, a pub recommended in the real ale guide. After a long drive to this village in the back of beyond it was discovered The Old Crown was closed on Wednesdays. The Mill Inn at Mungrisdale served as a substitute for an enjoyable lunch before the shops of Keswick were visited for as long as could be tolerated. After much debate and a long walk in the rain, the group visited the "famous" Pencil Museum in Keswick. The length of time spent in the museum was dictated by the continuing rain rather than by any fascination for pencils, but before readers draw their own conclusions it must be said that the museum was surprisingly interesting.

After returning to Troutbeck the customary visit was paid to the Inn for a pre-prandial refreshment. Tom was berating Andrew for having failed to provide HP sauce to accompany the mince which was on the evening's menu back at the cottage so the landlady at the Inn was asked if she had any sachets of the stuff which she might like to donate. She did better than that, returning with a full bottle, asking only that it be returned at the end of the week. Dinner was, therefore, eaten in peace.

The weather forecast for Thursday was for a dry, bright start with heavy rain arriving during the afternoon. Fortunately the hill chosen for the day's activity was Blencathra, a fine hill only a few miles from Mell Fell View, and by 9am the group was leaving the car park at the Scales Inn for the easy walk up to the tarn below Sharp Edge, reputedly the most interesting ascent route. The cottage had an excellent library, including many of Wainwright's guides, so the BSSMC had arrived at the foot of the rocky ridge armed with Wainwright's wonderful description, as follows:-

"Sharp Edge is a rising crest of naked rock, of sensational and spectacular appearance, a breaking wave carved in stone. The sight of it at close quarters is sufficient to make a beholder about to tackle it forget all other worries, even a raging toothache. The crest itself is sharp enough for shaving (the former name was Razor Edge) and can be traversed only à cheval at some risk of damage to tender parts. There is one awkward place, calling for a shuffle off a sloping slab on to a knife edge; countless posteriors have imparted a high polish to this spot."

On seeing the Edge and having read the description Rod elected for an easier route to the summit while the three others enjoyed the very airy scramble, made all the more interesting by a very strong, gusty wind. Rejoining Rod at the summit another strange celebration took place; over many years the need to carry some form of "emergency rations" had been drummed into Andrew. Fortunately no such occasion had arisen so his bar of Kendal Mint Cake had lain, unopened, in his rucksack for many years. On a summit overlooking Keswick it seemed appropriate to open and eat the said bar, with Andrew insisting it be shared. It was consumed with due ceremony and seemed surprisingly fresh.

The weather forecast proved accurate and as the group descended by Scales Fell rain was threatening. A most enjoyable 4 hour day was rounded off with a visit to the Scales Inn.

That left ample time to prepare for the second BSSMC annual dinner of the week, another excellent meal in the Troutbeck Inn. The borrowed bottle of HP sauce was returned.

Sadly, this chapter must end with an anti-climax. It was later discovered that there are two further summits in the Lake District which are classed officially as "3000 ft tops furth of Scotland", Ill Crag and Broad Crag, both of which are part of the Scafell Pike ridge. On the day of their visit, the BSSMC had been unaware of this, entirely due to a lack of proper research, so will have to make a return visit some day to legitimately claim "compleation of the Furths".

Chapter 34

Full Circle

The previous two years had seen several boxes ticked; the 30th anniversary of the BSSMC, the thirtieth annual expedition of the BSSMC and "compleation" of the 3000 ft tops furth of Scotland by Andrew, Graham and Tom (or so they thought at the time). It was inevitable that thoughts would return to Graham's list of incompleat (if that's the opposite of "compleat") Munros, a list which seemed to grow longer each year as he continued to verify where he had been in his younger days before becoming involved with those daft enough to actually count and record summits.

One constant remained, however – the six remote Munros in Fisherfield. That thought was pushed to one side yet again in 2010 and the easier option of a few Glenshee summits was resurrected, summits which had been options for Graham's "final" Munros. But a visit to Knoydart was also required, to climb Luinne Bheinn and Meall Buidhe. Few mountaineering folk would put Glenshee and Knoydart together in a single trip – but that is just the way of the BSSMC, so planning began, with the usual difficulty of identifying mutually acceptable dates.

The assembly point for the expedition was an unusual one, the premises of the Scotch Malt Whisky Society in Leith. Tom was arriving in Leith on the morning of 1st July, having been working on board a ship which had been on a trip round the British Isles. Tom would baulk at it being called a "cruise" as the ships he works on are a bit too exclusive for such a vulgar term to be applied. Anyway, Alastair collected Tom from his ship, Andrew arrived with a car full of supplies, Roderick arrived by car from Manchester and the four had an excellent lunch of haggis, neeps and tatties. With three drivers in the group, only Tom was able to enjoy several cask strength Malts. After lunch, Graham was met at Haymarket Station and three cars headed for Braemar and the Braemar Lodge Bunkhouse, the base for the first four nights. Paul arrived by car later that evening.

Weather forecasts were to be of particular importance this week in determining which hills would be on the agenda. The five day forecast suggested very changeable weather so the group relied heavily on the various forecasts available via interweb phone things, or whatever they are called. Things looked promising for the first day and a half, before going downhill.

The most challenging route, in terms of distance, was Carn an Righ and Beinn Iutharn Mhor so this was chosen for Friday. Cars were parked at the Dalmunzie House Hotel, shortening the day by around three miles, for a fee of £2 per car. It was fortunate Friday had been chosen as the hotel was being taken over for the weekend for a family birthday party and public parking was to be suspended – those three extra miles make such a difference on a long day.

The walk up Gleann Taitneach was most enjoyable, with fine weather offering good views and a sighting of one of the largest herds of deer ever encountered by the BSSMC – many hundreds of deer spread over a vast area of hillside. Unlike the previous visit by "The Happy Wanderers" in1986 the group did not walk together. Unsurprisingly, Graham set the pace and it became apparent he did not intend to stop for a break until reaching Loch nan Eun, about five miles from the hotel and some 450 metres higher. Lunch over, the group discussed who would be doing what. Graham, Andrew and Paul ascended Carn an Righ before heading over to Beinn Iuthern Mhor to meet the others who had gone directly there from the loch and were on their way down – it was a bit too cold and windy to be hanging around for long. As usual, everyone made their own way down to the loch, by various routes. After a re-grouping at the loch the long walk down the glen again afforded excellent views.

The forecast for Saturday suggested a sunny but windy morning with heavy showers in the afternoon, so the plan for a short, easy day fitted well. Carn Aosda was followed by the pleasant walk out to Carn a Gheodh but, with strengthening wind and increasing cloud, only Andrew and Graham took in the Cairnwell, something of a dump when not covered in snow and being used for ski-ing. So the hills that had been reserved for Graham's compleation were no longer on his "still to do" list. On return to the bunkhouse there was an incredibly heavy rain shower developing to huge hailstones – it would have been extremely unpleasant on the hill.

As Paul was returning home next day, the annual dinner was held on the Saturday night. Braemar offered a limited choice of venues (the Invercauld Arms was investigated and quickly dismissed – it appeared to have become a staging post for a convoy of buses full of predominantly English geriatrics talking very loudly about haggis and kilts. Food didn't seem high on their agenda). After a vote it was decided to cross the car park from the bunkhouse to the dining room of the Braemar Lodge Hotel for what turned out to be an excellent meal. Incidentally, Graham didn't have scampi or even fish and the duck proved popular.

Sunday dawned wet and miserable and Paul left after breakfast. It was a festering day for the others, although quite an active fester. Mar Lodge was having an open day, so that was the first stop. The Royal Lochnagar distillery didn't open until the afternoon, so there was a visit to Ballater for lunch, a stroll and a lengthy visit to the second hand bookshop before returning to the distillery for the tour and some purchases.

The other activity during the first few days had been visits to the bar in the Fife Arms to watch football. The World Cup was taking place in South Africa and most of the male English geriatrics in town wanted to watch it, despite the fact that England were already out of the tournament having been defeated by Germany, so the bar was unusually busy. From a BSSMC perspective England's failure to progress meant it was un-necessary to support any particular team, although there remained a soft spot for the Germans.

Roderick was leaving on Monday to spend a few days with his parents in Leven so he offered to clear up as the remaining four left early to drive to Mallaig for the onward trip to Knoydart. The ferry from Mallaig to Inverie didn't sail at weekends so the week's itinerary called for a midweek trip. Arriving at Mallaig in time for lunch, the only difficulty was deciding which restaurant/café would be selected for the fish and chips, the only meal in town. Making a collective decision has never been a BSSMC strong point but the chosen venue (isn't it strange how the first place considered is usually the one eventually selected?) produced excellent haddock, chips, bread and butter and tea (for Graham read Coke). Having parked the cars on the outskirts of town and with rucksacks packed, the BSSMC was Knoydart bound by ferry at 2.15pm.

Two nights had been booked in the Knoydart Foundation bunkhouse, which provided extremely comfortable accommodation, so the two hills had to be tackled on the Tuesday if at all possible. Lengthy studies of the weather forecasts suggested Tuesday morning would start with low cloud and light rain, followed by a clearer spell in the afternoon, followed by rain later in the day. This proved to be very accurate. The long walk up to the Mam Barrisdale, along the bank of the swollen Inverie River, was very wet underfoot and very damp overhead. Conditions at the top of the pass were extremely unpleasant so there was only a very brief stop for some food before tackling the soggy path, in places little better than a water course, to the summit of Luinne Bheinn. Conditions at the summit improved gradually as lunch was taken and on the way across to Meall Buidhe the sky cleared as forecast, to give good views in a drying wind. Visibility failed to assist Andrew and Tom's memories of these hills from 1979. They found nothing recognisable and began to wonder if they had ever actually been there at all – of course they had!! The wind increased as they made their way down a long spur to the boggy ground of the broad valley bellow. By this time, with rain appearing again, there was little point in trying to keep feet dry so it was an unpleasant final few miles back to the bunkhouse.

As wet clothes were lifted on to a huge pulley above a wood burning stove, another occupant of the bunkhouse, a young Englishman of short stature, said he had been on the same hills and only slightly ahead of the BSSMC. The fact that he had not been spotted at any point during the day led the BSSMC to doubt if he had actually been there. He was on the brink of "compleation" himself, with only a handful of summits left. With hindsight, the BSSMC didn't treat him as courteously as they might have, i.e. by doubting his integrity and not inviting him to join them in the pub later. Amazingly, Andrew came across the young man again several months later on a flight from Edinburgh to London. He was returning from a trip north during which he had completed his final Munro, this time with friends and the obligatory party.

An advance booking had been made for Tuesday night for dinner at The Old Forge, reputedly the remotest pub in Britain with no road access. The booking proved necessary as a large party was dining. This group turned out to be a party of school children from a Rudolf Steiner school in England who had walked to Inverie from Glenfinnan, camping along the way. The omens didn't look good as the 16 and 17 year old pupils queued noisily at the bar, but they settled down as they ate, while the BSSMC shared a table with an elderly couple by the name of Creed. It transpired that Mrs Creed, a lecturer in physiotherapy, knew several friends of Alastair's and John Creed knew an acquaintance of Andrew's in Peebles. The Creeds were the parents of the Turner Prize winner, Martin Creed. John Creed had been a lecturer at Glasgow School of Art and is well respected in his own right– he had made the gates for the revamped Kelvingrove Art Gallery amongst other significant works. After an excellent dinner – local seafood, venison and beef, the crowded pub was entertained to an evening of singing by the Rudolf Steiner pupils, to an extremely high standard. Their alcohol consumption was both responsible and minimal, if perhaps of dubious legality. The evening's events rounded off what had been a memorable day.

The return boat trip from Knoydart to Mallaig next day was rough with strong winds and squally showers. There was time for Andrew and Tom to reflect on the years which had passed since their first visit to Knoydart in 1979. Some 31 years later they and Roderick had still managed to get out on some hills together – their original intention when they set off on that first annual trip. Graham is now only six Munros short of "compleation" and although his remaining summits will be a challenge for his older friends there is a determination that he will get there. Alastair always tries to join the annual expedition as his work pattern permits. Paul has racked up a good number of Munros while snowboarding remains his preferred action sport. Gavin and Mike have dipped in and out over the years. Overall, the BSSMC seems to have survived remarkably well.

But this written record of the BSSMC has reached a point where it needs to come to a close, or it may never see the light of day. Although the number of members may be small, there is a will to carry on the annual expedition. Hopefully, 2011 will be about Graham's "compleation", 2 012 may see a trip to Dumfries and Galloway to enable Andrew to "compleat" the "Donalds" and who knows what beyond that – new blood, geriatric meanderings, or just meeting over a dram to reminisce? Perhaps future exploits will appear in Volume 2 of "The Bearsden Secret Society Mountaineering Club."

The only thing left to do on the journey home was to call in at the West End Hotel in Fort William for a very familiar lunch. Graham probably had scampi.

Chapter 35

P.S. Graham's "Compleation"

This ought to have been the first chapter of Volume 2 of the BSSMC's exploits but events of 2011 are considered worthy of inclusion. The main question on readers' minds will surely be "Did Graham "compleat" the Munros?" The short answer is, yes, but let's look at how.

For one reason or another no one seemed to be available for a trip to Shenavall bothy to climb "The Fisherfield Six" in 2011 and there was a concern that if left much longer such a trip might never happen. But Andrew and Graham were able to make the trip, even if Andrew had some doubts as to whether he was really up to it, so arrangements were made to travel north on Sunday 12th June.

Unfortunately, attempts to find an early evening bar meal in the Dundonnell area were thwarted by that traditional Highland problem – "We're closed, at least until much later". After a lengthy wait, during which rucksacks were packed, the bar in the Dundonnell Hotel opened and the pair ate before an evening walk in to Shenavall.

During a summer which was to turn out to be the wettest on record in Scotland, the weather forecast gave little cause for optimism so it looked as though it might be necessary to spend more than a couple of days at Shenavall. Rucksacks were therefore heavy with provisions for the walk in. It was late evening as they set off up the good track which goes over the hill to Strath na Sealga. At a high bealach they joined the much more sketchy and very wet path for the final few miles to the bothy. On arrival they found the bothy completely unoccupied and considerably upgraded since previous visits. The loft had been completely re-floored and a proper staircase erected, giving a much larger sleeping area upstairs. For the first night, however, Graham and Andrew elected to sleep in the downstairs room which turned out to be rather damp and draughty. (They moved up to the much drier and warmer loft for the remainder of their stay).

As forecast, it rained heavily all night and next morning making the crossing of the river extremely dangerous. Checking the swollen river several times, Andrew and Graham agreed it was just not feasible to wade across so the day was spent in the bothy, trying to keep warm and reading to pass the time.

Monday was dry and much brighter and the weather promised to hold for the day. With the forecast for Tuesday suggesting rain later in the day, Andrew suggested that Graham might want to tackle all 6 tops in one long day, although he knew he would hold Graham back if he accompanied him. They agreed that Graham would traverse the first three tops himself and Andrew would meet him on Beinn Tarsuinn, the point on the route furthest away from the bothy, then accompany him on his final two summits, A'Mhaighdean and Ruadh Stac Mor.

Having waded the river safely, Graham set off over the first three summits at his usual rapid pace while Andrew walked up the long valley of Gleann na Muice to meet Graham near the summit of Beinn Tarsuinn, remarkably close to the time they had agreed. They dropped down to the bealach which led to the long, broad spur on to the summit of A'Mhaighdean. Andrew was really struggling but was determined to witness Graham's "compleation" so Graham was kept waiting before the pair enjoyed the magnificent views from the summit of this very remote Munro. From there, the route led down to a bealach where there is a small cave which can be used as a bivouac in emergencies, then up the steep, loose side of Ruadh Stac Mor.

At the summit of Ruadh Stac Mhor Graham seemed totally underwhelmed by his achievement while Andrew was relieved just to be there and delighted that Graham had finally "compleated" the Munros. Two other walkers were present to witness the fairly muted celebrations, some 23 year old, cask strength Glenfarclas and the obligatory summit photos.

The long walk back to Shenavall through the remote centre of the Fisherfield Forest was fairly uneventful and the fording of the two rivers presented no great difficulties. The pair enjoyed a welcome can of beer back at the bothy, followed by a meal cooked on Graham's trusty Trangia stove which had been resurrected for this trip. Evening celebrations were limited to a few drams

The bothy remained quiet, with only two others present that night. They, too, were planning to tackle the six tops in one day en route to "compleation". (Just a week or so later it was announced that, following a review of its height, Beinn a'Chlaidheimh was no longer a Munro, but as it is difficult to avoid it on the route most folk will still take it in). Apart from this pair, the only other visitor had been a long distance walker calling in to dry off and cook a meal during the wet Monday. Having met their objective Andrew and Graham decided they would make a leisurely return to Dundonnell on Tuesday , taking the longer but drier track along the valley and up to the bealach. There, over lunch, they met another long distance walker who had started his walk in the Peak District and was finishing at John o' Groats. Before long, Andrew was to be very glad of his presence.

The car was now only two miles away down a good landrover track so Graham sped off with Andrew some way behind. With Graham out of sight, Andrew said goodbye to the long distance walker and set off down the track. After only a few minutes, on a steep but straightforward slope, Andrew's left foot slipped on some loose gravel and, with the weight of his ergonomically unsound, forty year old "Joe Brown" rucksack pulling him off balance, his right leg buckled underneath and behind him, accompanied by a loud "snap". On his back, like an overturned turtle, the excruciating pain Andrew was experiencing convinced him he had broken his leg. Unable to get to his feet, he struggled to haul himself to the side of the path to wait the arrival of the long distance walker who uttered that rhetorical question "Are you OK?"

It quickly became apparent that Andrew wasn't OK. The walker helped remove the rucksack and helped Andrew to his feet. The fact that he could stand with support suggested he hadn't broken his leg but he could barely take a step. It was agreed that the walker would carry on down to the car – he was going that way in any case – and alert Graham to the problem. Hopefully, Graham would come back up the path to carry Andrew's rucksack while Andrew would try to hobble down the path with the aid of his walking poles as best he could. To Andrew this seemed a better option than staying put and calling out the Mountain Rescue Team – that was too ignominious an end to the expedition to be considered.

To cut a painful story short, Graham's sleep in the car was disturbed by the walker knocking on the window and, despite being exhausted from his previous day's efforts, he hurried back up the track to meet his struggling companion. It took Andrew three hours of agony to walk/limp the two miles back to the car.

As both had been looking forward to a celebratory meal and possibly a comfortable night's accommodation locally, Andrew was reluctant to seek medical treatment that evening but Graham felt it was necessary. Driving, with considerable difficulty, to Raigmore Hospital in Inverness, the pair once again encountered the problem of finding somewhere to eat en route. After several abortive attempts to find somewhere open and serving reasonable food, the bar meal at Muir of Ord was fine but it was hardly the celebration Graham deserved.

On then to Raigmore hospital where the wait in Accident and Emergency was brief and the medical staff excellent. While Andrew's leg was being x-rayed, the diagnosis being torn quadriceps and possibly tendon damage, then being put in a back-slab (an ankle to buttock plaster left slightly open at the front) Graham, with help from an A&E receptionist, was arranging overnight accommodation at the nearby Raigmore Motel – at a discount price for referrals from the hospital. On crutches, Andrew managed to negotiate the few steps into the bar at the motel and the pair enjoyed a quiet drink.

Having spent a surprisingly comfortable night and enjoyed a hearty cooked breakfast, arrangements were made for Graham to be named on Andrew's car insurance. He then drove Andrew back to Peebles before being abandoned to make his own way back to Glasgow by public transport.

Graham's celebration dinner with the other BSSMC members will have to be put on ice until the next annual expedition. His round of his final 6 Munros had involved a walk of 16 miles and 7260 feet (2200 metres) of ascent so surely he deserves something better than a plate of scampi.

To be continued...........?

BSSMC Compleation Party 1997